Kicking Back

For Diane —
Bless your heart!

All best —
John

John Shelton Reed

Kicking Back

Further Dispatches from the South

University of Missouri Press

Columbia London

Library of Congress Cataloging-in-Publication Data

Reed, John Shelton.

   Kicking back : further dispatches from the South / John Shelton Reed.

    p.   cm.

   ISBN 0-8262-1004-X

   1. Southern States—Social life and customs. I. Title

F216.2.R417   1995

975—dc20   94-47492

                                                   CIP

Designer: Stephanie Foley
Typesetter: BOOKCOMP
Printer and binder: Thomson-Shore, Inc.
Typefaces: Cheltenham and Times

To kindred spirits,
known and unknown

Contents

Preface

T he pieces collected in this book speak of many things: of the Civil War and deconstruction, of flush times and flush toilets, of collard greens and kings. (There are at least passing references to three kings—Jesus, Elvis, and Richard Petty—and an entire essay on *Martin Luther* King.) They hang together, if at all, as an assortment of anecdotes and reflections having to do with what the South and Southerners are up to these days.

To be sure, some are actually about California and Vermont and England. But they're about those places as seen through Southern eyes—that is, through mine. To pretend to speak for the South would be silly, not to mention presumptuous. But I don't pretend, either, that where I sit doesn't affect the view. Maybe my view's enough like yours that you'll like it, or different enough that you'll find it exotic, but I hope at least you won't find it boring. If you do, I've really failed, because Lord knows the South is an *interesting* place, these days.

One of the interesting things about it is the persistence of a good many peculiarly Southern characteristics, hard to measure in any scientific way, but even harder to deny. The first section of this book examines some of those characteristics: things like distinctive manners, a sense of place, a fondness for grand-sounding titles, a narrative conversational style. Most of these traits I find engaging, some of them have served Southerners well, and I'm glad to see that they seem to be surviving. Some of my observations here—those on manners, in particular—echo those of W. J. Cash in *The Mind of the South*, the fiftieth anniversary of which was the occasion for the very first of these pieces.

"Southrons, Hear Your Country Call You," the title of my second section, is of course from the "official" version of "Dixie"—the one that never caught on. (The next line is "Up, lest worse than death befall you.") I suppose nearly everyone who's read this far knows

Faulkner's line about the past not being dead, not even past: the essays in Section II treat the sometimes perplexing question of what to do with the South's history. The first treats the mint julep, and an appeal to preserve that historic Southern potation is probably innocent enough, but when we turn to some of the South's other traditions the water quickly gets deeper and more treacherous. The next several essays try to muddy that water for some symbols and historical memories linked to the Confederacy, suggesting that these matters are more complicated than partisans on either side are likely to admit. (It's a thankless task, but somebody's got to do it.) The last essay in the section, on the Atlanta Olympics, laments what I see as a tendency to "put the past behind us" by simply ignoring it.

Section III, "Fools' Names and Fools' Faces . . . ," analyzes, appreciates, autopsies, or otherwise pokes at a few Southerners whose names have oft appeared in public places. All of them are politicians except Martin Luther King Jr.—and by some reckonings I guess he was, too. Louisiana is represented here by one piece on Earl Long and another on David Duke and Edwin Edwards. Just as those of us from other Southern states are supposed to thank God for Mississippi when the subject of poverty comes up, so we can thank Him for Louisiana when the talk turns to politics. But other states have their own political points of interest. North Carolina, for instance, offers Senator Jesse Helms, whose face-off with Harvey Gantt in a 1990 Senate race I found instructive, and Texas supplied both the incumbent in the 1992 presidential election and, in Ross Perot, the most interesting challenger. Why Perot is interesting is the subject of one of these essays; why Bill Clinton and Al Gore are not is the subject of another.

The fourth section is a hodgepodge of reflections on questions of the day: one on the pressing business of state mottoes and mascots, a couple on what can be loosely characterized as environmentalism, three on "political correctness" (I am a university professor, after all), and two that ask, in effect, what ever happened to federalism. In this and the preceding section you'll probably notice my politics, if you haven't already. Yeah, they tend to be conservative. Some folks have a problem with that, but, as we say in East Tennessee, tough—well, never mind what we say in East Tennessee.

Section V reports on travels—to New England and old, to Montreal and Santa Fe, to Yosemite and the Grand Canyon, to West Texas and, notably, northern California, where my wife and I lived for a year. One way or another, most of these pieces are reflections on what has come to be called (by people I generally don't much care for) "multiculturalism." I've always been in favor of it. Still am. Seems to me if someplace is different, you should be glad that it's there. If you like it, you can visit; if you don't, at least it's somewhere else. Much as I like the South, I don't want the whole world to look Southern: if nothing else, it would take much of the pleasure out of going home.

Anyway, in Section VI, I do go home, back behind the Kudzu Curtain for a variety of truly Southern experiences: a barbecue cook-off in Memphis, a stock-car race in Darlington, a War Between the States reenactment in North Carolina, a Kappa Alpha "convivium" and some church services in Jackson, a tent meeting (of sorts) in Little Rock. I hope you enjoy them. I sure did.

A word about this book's title: A while back I wrote a book called *Whistling Dixie*, and when I was trying to think what to call this one, my wife suggested *Same Song, Second Verse*. I thought that was just about perfect: the words are different, but the tune *is* pretty much the same. My friends at the University of Missouri Press really didn't like that title, though, so in deference to them I came up with another— but if you're among the majority of readers who didn't read *Whistling Dixie*, it's a lot like this, OK?

You say *Kicking Back*'s ambiguous? That's right.

Acknowledgments

I have right much thanking to do, starting with Jane and Greg Shaw, my sister and her husband, for getting me the Memphis barbecue gig and putting me up while I did it. Fetzer Mills, my ex-student, poker-playing buddy, and font of political wisdom, appears in several of these chapters; I'm especially grateful to him for serving as my interpreter and native guide at Darlington.

Some of these essays were written while I was visiting Millsaps College as the Eudora Welty Professor of Southern Studies, and I thank Robert King, Suzanne Marrs, and the many other hospitable folks down yonder. Others I wrote while a fellow of the Center for Advanced Study in the Behavioral Sciences in Palo Alto. (Needless to say, they do not necessarily—or even probably—reflect the opinions of my friends and colleagues at that splendid institution.) But most were written between classes and committee meetings at the University of North Carolina at Chapel Hill, which I've found a haven of blessing and peace (mostly) for twenty-five years now. I honestly can't think of any place I'd rather have been.

"Preaching a Revival" is reprinted with permission from *Southern Living* (Copyright by Southern Living Inc., June 1994 [thanks to Dianne Young]). "Bubba Hubbub" originally appeared in *Reason* magazine (thanks to Rick Henderson and Virginia Postrel), and parts of "A Mind of the South" come from my review of Bruce Clayton's *W. J. Cash: A Life*, in the *Raleigh News and Observer* (thanks to Michael Skube). Those publications hold the copyrights on those materials, and I appreciate their permission to include them here. I also thank the University Press of Mississippi for permission to use some portions of "Class Dismissed" that come from *"The Mind of the South* and Southern Distinctiveness," a paper that I read at the Chancellor's Symposium on Southern History at the University of Mississippi and that was later published in Charles W. Eagles, ed., *The Mind of the South: Fifty Years Later* (1992).

Nearly everything else originally appeared as "Letters from the Lower Right" in *Chronicles: A Magazine of American Culture*, which holds the copyright. I'm perpetually indebted to Kate Dalton, Ted Pappas, and my other *Chronicles* colleagues, past and present, and especially to Tom Fleming, that doughty magazine's editor. The views expressed here are not always his (as he has forcefully made known to me on occasion), but he has never even hesitated to publish them, despite my oft-stated belief that an editor ought to be held responsible for the contents of his magazine. I'm grateful to Tom for suffering me gladly, to all appearances, and for what that implies.

This is, what, my fourth book with the University of Missouri Press? Thanks again to Beverly Jarrett and her talented staff, especially Gloria Thomas. And, as always, I'm grateful to Dale—and for much more than suggesting a great title.

I

The Mind of the South
(Still Crazy after All These Years)

A Mind of the South

February 10, 1991, was the fiftieth anniversary of the publication of *The Mind of the South*, W. J. Cash's classic and, in the event, only book. Probably because reading Cash was a formative experience for most members of the symposium-going class of Southerners, there were a number of gatherings to mark the occasion. As a matter of fact, there was one on February 10 at Wake Forest, Cash's alma mater. Alas, I missed it: I was in northern California for the year, cut off from my roots and also from such delightful perks of my profession as hanging out with a bunch of my friends and talking about one of my favorite books while drinking somebody else's Jack Daniel's.

As far as I can tell, the anniversary passed unremarked in the Golden West, although some of the local intelligentsia had a conference of their own the next weekend, something called the National Sexuality Symposium. I thought about venturing the $245 registration fee so I could write a column about it, but then I realized I didn't know who'd publish my discussion of techniques for extended orgasm or erotic filmmaking, much less whatever was said at the workshop on S&M for beginners. I am sorry to have missed the "erotic costume ball" at the San Francisco Airport Hilton, though; I had this *great* idea for a costume.

But back to W. J. Cash. You know, he really did write a strange book. One of the strangest things about it is that it's still read and discussed fifty years after it was written. After all, historians who don't agree about much of anything else do agree that as a historian Cash is—well, a good prose stylist. And even his prose isn't to everyone's taste these days. A saving remnant of my students share my taste for great rolling periods punctuated by snappy colloquialisms, but more of them seem to wish that Cash would just get to the point; they don't know what to highlight with their yellow markers.

Still, the book is widely read even when it hasn't been assigned. One day in a Buckinghamshire bookshop, for example, I spied a Confederate battle flag from across the room, on the cover of the British edition. And some of Cash's great broad-brush generalizations about the South have become almost conventional wisdom among college-educated Southerners, whether they know where the wisdom came from or not. Again and again in his book *A Turn in the South*,

V. S. Naipaul unwittingly paraphrases Cash by quoting his informants' "observations"—probably, in fact, repetitions of things that they read or heard as undergraduates.

It's true that many of these ideas weren't original with Cash, but he gave them popular currency. As Bruce Clayton shows in his biography of its author, *The Mind of the South* has demanded and received attention ever since its publication. It didn't sneak up on our notice like, say, James Agee's *Let Us Now Praise Famous Men* (published the same year but pretty much ignored until the 1960s); it was widely and favorably reviewed in both the popular and the academic press, North and South alike, and if its actual sales were disappointing—well, tell me about it. As Alfred Knopf tried to explain to Cash, that's what usually happens with serious works of nonfiction. (The book later sold very well indeed, in overseas and paperback editions, but by then Cash's widow had unwisely sold the author's rights to Knopf.)

But even if the book didn't make Cash much money, it made him an immediate literary celebrity. Many in 1941 saw *The Mind of the South* as an antidote for *Gone with the Wind*, published not long before. Cash had actually reviewed Margaret Mitchell's book and called it "sentimental" (than which there were few adjectives more damning in the mouth of someone who aspired to a tough, cynical, Menckenian style), but when Miss Mitchell invited the Cashes to dinner at the Piedmont Driving Club, the two writers hit it off famously, swapping stories and compliments. Not surprising, really: both moved in the New South's smart set and shared its tastes and assumptions. Besides, *sentimental* isn't exactly the right word for Peggy Mitchell's book, just as it's not exactly the wrong word for Jack Cash's: Cash's "man at the center" looks an awful lot like Gerald O'Hara.

After his book came out, Cash also visited and schmoozed with Carson McCullers, Lillian Smith, Ralph McGill, and (oddly) Karl Menninger. On the strength of his reviews, he got a Guggenheim fellowship, and he set off to Mexico to write a novel, stopping on the way to give the commencement address at the University of Texas. After a couple of weeks in Mexico he hanged himself, but more about that in a minute.

On the face of it, Cash was an unlikely literary giant. God knows he was a mess, as Clayton's book shows. Just a few years earlier, thirty-six years old, unmarried, and unable to hold a job for long, he had moved back to little Boiling Springs, North Carolina, to live with his parents. "Sleepy" (as his friends called him) was supposed to be working on his book, but he seemed to spend most of his time riding his bicycle, chopping wood, and dozing in the sun in front of the courthouse. His recurrent attacks of "neurasthenia" and "melancholia" were notorious; he also suffered from goiter and (secretly) from fears of impotence. He stayed up nights talking with an unemployed Baptist preacher, drank too much, smoked too much, and probably didn't eat his vegetables.

True, he had been a BMOC as a Wake Forest undergraduate, a campus character with his pipe and chewing tobacco, terrifying Meredith College girls with his fierce intellectuality, writing poems and short stories, reading H. L. Mencken, and imitating the master in crusading editorials for the school paper. But then he dropped out of law school ("you have to lie too much"). He didn't last as a college English teacher, either (most students were "satisfied with football, rah-rah, and Commerce A"). He wrote and burned several novels and collected rejection slips for his short stories. In a brief flurry of success in 1929–1930, he placed three iconoclastic essays on the South in Mencken's *American Mercury;* one, "The Mind of the South," won him a book contract with Knopf. Then it was back to dithering.

He wrote now and then for Charlotte newspapers, turned down offers of better newspaper jobs in Cleveland and New York for vague reasons of health, and edited a small-town weekly before his health made him give that up, too. (Clayton concludes that Cash suffered recurrent depression, brought on by hyperthyroidism and endocrine imbalance, and aggravated by hard drinking.) Cash's parents weren't well off, but when his doctor recommended rest and travel they staked him to a European tour. He loved the Parisian vie bohème and burst into tears at Chartres, then returned to Boiling Springs, his parents, and his unfinished manuscript.

So everyone was surprised (it seems not least his publisher) when he finished *The Mind of the South.* Yet during his seemingly unproductive and aimless twenties and thirties, Cash had been observing and thinking about what he saw: the Gastonia strike, the Ku Klux Klan, political demagoguery, lynchings, the Dayton "monkey trial"—it all comes out in the book, and it's not a pretty picture.

Those Southerners who wanted unstinting loyalty to the homeland weren't pleased. Donald Davidson didn't like the book at all and said so in one of the few negative reviews the book received. (Characteristically gallant, Davidson regretted that the news of Cash's suicide reached him too late for him to pull the review.) I hate to disagree with Mr. Davidson on this matter, but I do. Twenty-odd years ago, C. Vann Woodward wrote that "social scientists, especially sociologists," seem to have "a special affinity" for *The Mind of the South*. Maybe that's it.

Anyway, it's true that Cash hated a lot about the South. Occasionally he was imagining things, sometimes he was just being fashionable, but often he was right. And it's obvious that he loved the place, too, because what started out as a smart-aleck essay for Mencken's magazine wound up as a book that any reader should recognize as a cry from the heart.

It's easy to criticize Cash's picture of the South. His almost completely unsympathetic treatment of Southern religion, for instance, strikes me as perversely obtuse. Even when he gets it pretty much right—as I think he does with Southern individualism—he tends to go overboard. But that almost doesn't matter now. Cash's South may not correspond perfectly or even very well to the real one, but it's certainly a fascinating place. About the accuracy of Cash's descriptions and the validity of his explanations scholars differ and, I guess, always will, but as a work of the imagination *The Mind of the South* is a remarkable achievement, far better, as Clayton suggests, than any novel Cash was ever likely to write.

Vann Woodward observed once that Cash himself "was merely illustrating once more that ancient Southern trait that he summed up in the word 'extravagant' "—and that's exactly what some of us like about the book: the sound of its words, the sweep of its history, the boldness and the flamboyance and the very exaggeration of its characterizations. ("Softly; do you not hear behind that the gallop of Jeb Stuart's cavalrymen?")

And that suicide? Some said that Cash was driven to it by worry about the Southern reaction to his criticism, that he was thus a victim himself of what he called the "savage ideal" of conformity. Can we see his self-destruction as a last extravagant Q.E.D.?

No. Nearly all Southern reviewers liked the book. The real story is less ironic, but even sadder. Shortly before his death he had been hearing nonexistent voices, and he thought the Nazis were out to get him. Clayton concludes that Cash probably killed himself during an episode of delirium tremens caused by involuntary alcohol withdrawal, the result of a severe case of Montezuma's revenge. For once in his life, Jack Cash wasn't thinking about the South.

Class Dismissed

A while back my friend Dick, a history professor here, was riding in a Long Island airport limousine when it stopped to pick up another passenger, an elderly lady burdened with luggage and confronted by a garden gate that wouldn't open. After watching her struggle for a while, Dick got out and gave her a hand. When they were settled in the car the lady thanked him. The driver (who had watched everything from behind the wheel) said, "He's from the South."

I find that a delicious story, not least because Dick is a Midwesterner who came to North Carolina via Harvard and Oxford and he's about as Southern as—oh, say, as T. S. Eliot. That story suggests how careful we should be about generalizing, but it also tells us that, despite all the incursions of Northern folks and Northern ways, people still think Southern manners are different.

And of course they are different. A case in point: you know the National Public Radio program "Car Talk"? (Two genial brothers dispense automotive advice mixed with bad puns and insults? That one?) The hosts are absolutely typical Boston-Italian wise guys, maybe smarter than a dozen others I've known, that's all, and they habitually practice what someone once called "participatory listening"—what we in the South call *interrupting*. Consequently, "Car Talk" usually sounds something like a two-man McLaughlin Group, which can be disconcerting if you don't understand how to keep score. South Carolina Public Radio once dropped the program because listeners found the chatter intolerably rude. (Later the program was picked up again: either South Carolinians are learning, or there are more Yankees in the Palmetto State than I thought.)

Such differences can lead to misunderstanding. As Americans continue their flight to the South from the regions that they've already ruined, much of the low-intensity conflict between Yankee settlers and

Southern aborigines reflects this. Just the other day, for instance, a student was telling me about her new neighbors, a Jewish couple from Los Angeles, who were mightily offended when a new acquaintance asked them casually where they go to church. In the South, this is still a standard gambit, no offense intended, just a way of figuring out who you're dealing with. "We're Jewish" is a perfectly satisfactory response. But apparently Angelenos feel it's none of our business.

But, you know, Californians have their own intrusive ways. When we lived out yonder, for instance, people often asked what I do for exercise, a question *I* find offensive. For starters, it's embarrassing: coughing a lot is about the extent of my exercise program these days. Besides, I tend to agree with Robert Frost: "After babyhood self-improvement becomes a private matter. Physical mental or moral, please attend to it where I cant see you if you care to avoid my disgust." (That's the old New Englander's own punctuation, or lack of it.)

Anyway, Southern manners really are still different, and Southerners usually think they're *better*, too. But Southern manners can get you in trouble outside the South. Once I was talking to a couple of friends on a corner at DuPont Circle, in Washington, when a sorry-looking black wino edged up to us and stood there, not saying a word. My friends, city boys, ignored him. I tried to, but finally I just couldn't stand pretending that the guy simply . . . *wasn't there*, so I made eye contact, knowing perfectly well that it was a mistake.

"Excuse me, sir," he said, "but can you help a homeless individual?" (In D.C. even the bums use the approved euphemisms.)

Well, the "excuse me, sir" did it. This guy's mama had raised him right. His manners (and mine) scored him my pocket change.

Another example: in *Southern Ladies and Gentlemen*, Florence King writes about the trials of a Southern woman in New York, "When you rattle off a standard Southern thank-you—'Oh, you're just so nice, I don't know what I'd *do* without you!'—the Northern man *believes you!* He believes you so much that he follows you home."

I know what she means. I've actually had a similar experience. On an international flight a couple of years ago, I'd been talking with a cute little Japanese-American flight attendant and was startled to be asked for my phone number. All I'd done was *chat* (honest). I didn't want to be rude, but I'm happily married, so I just made up a number. Besides, he wasn't my type—which is female, for starters. (Sorry. Couldn't resist telling it that way.)

Anyway, these days more and more Southerners have to deal with non-Southerners, and being misunderstood may in time make us as curt, abrupt, and no-nonsense as New Yorkers. But that would be a shame. Our manners have served us well, and not just by making everyday dealings with strangers more pleasant. As W. J. Cash recognized fifty years ago, in *The Mind of the South*, manners are one reason the "yoke" of class has "weighed but lightly" in these parts.

Now, Cash didn't deny that there are class distinctions in the South; indeed, he emphasized them, like the aspiring 1930s intellectual he was. But he insisted that there had been an "almost complete disappearance of economic and social focus on the part of the masses." That's typically Cashian overstatement, but can we agree that there hasn't been anywhere near as much class consciousness in the South as you might expect?

Cash argued that the "essential kernel" of "the famous Southern manner" was simply the "kindliness and easiness" of Southern backcountry life, and he observed that the Southern etiquette of class has softened the distinction between rich and poor, just as the old etiquette of race continually emphasized the gulf of caste. Among whites, he wrote, the manners governing relations between the classes have served as "a balance wheel in the Southern social world and . . . a barrier against the development of bitterness"—or, you could as easily say, against the development of class consciousness.

In the Old South, Cash maintained, the white yeoman seldom encountered "naked hauteur." The gentleman "patronize[d] him in such fashion that . . . he seemed not to be patronized at all but actually deferred to." The Civil War, in Cash's view, meant only that "the captains knew [even] better how to handle the commoner, to steer expertly about his recalcitrance, to manipulate him without ever arousing his jealous independence." And the rise of industry meant merely that "the old personal easy relations" of the countryside were brought indoors:

> The [textile] baron knew these workmen familiarly as Bill and Sam and George and Dick, or as Lil and Sal and Jane and Lucy. More, he knew their pedigrees and their histories. More still,

with that innocent love of personal detail native to Southerners, he kept himself posted as to their lives as they were lived under his wing; knew their little adventures and scandals and hopes and loves and griefs and joys.

This particular description goes on, and on, and it's easy to make fun of it, but surely we can allow Cash some license in describing the human face of paternalism, since he was unsparing in his treatment of its defects. In any case, this is not just a flight of romanticism, grotesquely applied to the textile mill. Cash was on to something.

I won't soon forget what a Mississippi buddy said one time when he stopped off to see us on his way home from a sociological convention in the Northeast. Over bourbon he said that he'd noticed something interesting about how some sociologists dealt with the staff of the convention hotel. "Damn Marxists," he said, "go on and on about the *workers*—and they treat the help like dirt."

Partly, of course, this is just the ordinary arrogance of Yankee intellectuals who, deep down, really don't buy into all that dignity of labor stuff. One day at lunch I was talking educational policy with one of the breed, who clinched his argument by saying, "If kids don't get a good education, they'll wind up like *him*"—nodding scornfully in the direction of a cafeteria worker.

I didn't know what to say. We both saw this man almost every day. He did his undemanding job cheerfully and well, and he was making an honest living, which is more than can be said for some tenured professors. It had never occurred to me that he was a bad example, but obviously my colleague despised the man for his insignificance.

Even if he hadn't, though, his manners might have suggested that he did. From a Southern point of view, many Yankees, Marxist or otherwise, treat *everyone* like dirt. And if you're working for one, those manners rub your face in the fact of your subordination.

Not long ago, my hometown was buzzing with the story of the Yankee newcomer who took a work crew to task for some fault with their work. The workers simply packed up their tools and left him sputtering in mid-criticism. "Sonofabitch wants to boss you around like he owns you" was thought to be sufficient explanation.

That's a significant phrase, isn't it? "Like he *owns* you." As legatees of a slave society—whether our ancestors were on the top, bottom, or side—Southerners may have a special understanding of the importance of independence, dignity, and pride. It makes sense that the fictive equality among white men should have been embodied in manners that didn't bring into question the other's worth or self-respect.

Those manners seem to be outlasting the conditions that gave rise to them—indeed, they're usually extended now to Southern blacks, most of whom seem willing to return the favor—but they are threatened, and not just by Northern newcomers. In fact, they were already threatened in 1940, as Cash recognized. He was deadly on the imported "Yankee cult of the Great Executive," which appealed to "the vanity especially of the young men who had been educated in the Northern business schools." Well, we have our own business schools now.

But there are still Southern enterprises run on the old principles, and those principles still shape the expectations of many Southern workers. A while back I took a class on a field trip to one of the few remaining family-owned textile mills in North Carolina. The trip had been arranged far in advance, but we arrived to find the place virtually shut down. The entire managerial staff and all but a skeleton crew of workers had gone to the funeral of a retired weave-room worker. Don't look for that mill to be unionized anytime soon.

A stone's throw away, in Winston-Salem, we recently witnessed an instructive cultural conflict, when Reynolds Tobacco merged with Nabisco and acquired a new management team. *Barbarians at the Gate*, the bestseller about the RJR-Nabisco leveraged buy-out, tells the story of Ross Johnson, the new Canadian CEO. Compared to the junk-bond sharks who eventually stripped him of his company and his job, Johnson comes off as a rather amiable buccaneer, just a guy out of the Nabisco sales division who liked to fly around the country in private jets and hang out with professional athletes, but he and his team of outsiders sadly misunderstood, and underestimated, the locals:

> The newcomers, Northerners almost to a man, stood out painfully at Reynolds. "It's not the end of the earth," they joked of Winston-Salem, "but you can see it from here." They mistook gentility for weakness, slowness of pace for lack of acumen, and

Southern accents for dim-wittedness. "They would treat brilliant people as backwater rubes," recalled [one] ad executive.

Johnson's *Great Executive style was also a striking change for RJR. Mr. R. J. Reynolds and his heirs hadn't exactly led lives of asceticism and self-denial, but they had been managers of the old-fashioned Southern variety. It was understood, for instance, that Reynolds executives drove nothing bigger than a Buick. When David Rockefeller came to Winston-Salem for a speech and asked for a limousine, there was not one to be found in the entire city. In the 1950s, one worker recalled, "I remember some mornings pulling up beside Mr. Whitaker [the president] in his little brown Studebaker. He'd give me a wave and I'd give him a wave back. We were going in to work together. We were all after the same thing."

Ross Johnson came to work by helicopter. You wonder why Winston-Salem never took to him?

Folks were especially cruel to Johnson's trophy wife, Laurie, a California Girl widely known as "Cupcake." (After she and her husband were given honorary degrees by a needy Florida college, she was known as "Dr. Cupcake.") When Johnson got even by moving his corporate headquarters to Atlanta, observing as he left that Winston-Salem was too "bucolic," bumpers blossomed with stickers saying "Proud to Be Bucolic."

Sure, there is deference in the South to men of high standing, but it can't be taken for granted, and it depends on a measure of self-deprecation. Cash got that exactly right. Southerners usually treat each other as equals, whatever our private opinions. That is, unless we *want* to insult someone. Someone like Ross Johnson. But that's another story.

The Honorable Gentleman from New York

It shouldn't be news to anyone that middle-aged professors with conservative politics are rare birds. Until recently, we've been almost as rare as black academics, and for pretty much the same reason: bright right-wingers can generally do better elsewhere. So it didn't go to my head a few years ago when I learned that the Reagan

White House was thinking of nominating me for the council of the National Endowment for the Humanities. I mean, how many Scholars for Reagan-Bush were there, after all?

Still, I was secretly a little proud. That is, until someone showed me a list of Jimmy Carter's appointees. And when the Reagan folks withdrew the nomination of a worthy fellow-nominee who had, over the years, guarded his tongue less assiduously than I, I recognized that the Democrats are not uniquely political. Call me naive, but I was disappointed to learn how much politics affects political appointments.

In my case, the White House sure was cautious. If the Reagan administration had been half as careful with its cabinet officers and Supreme Court nominees, it would have been spared some embarrassment. I had to fill out forms listing every organization I'd ever belonged to, every place I'd ever lived, and every time I'd left the country. (The dates of a trip to the Bahamas with my fishing buddies gave me trouble, until my wife reminded me that it was the weekend of Mother's Day, 1976. What a memory she has!) I calculated my net worth for the first time in my life, a depressing exercise, and started hearing from old friends I hadn't seen in years, who wanted to know why the FBI was asking about me.

Nobody asked me whether I'd ever smoked marijuana, but this was before that question became de rigueur for folks of my generation. I wonder, could I have come up with anything as classy as Bill Bennett's answer ("If I have any confessions to make, I'll make them to a priest"), or as bewildering as Marion Barry's ("Not to my knowledge")?

Anyway, in the fullness of time, a press release came from the White House, announcing my nomination. Its three paragraphs contained three errors of fact and a couple more of implication, but we conservatives aren't surprised when government screws up. I wasn't upset until the last line, which read, "Mr. Reed is a native of New York."

Well. Norman Podhoretz wrote once about the dirty little secrets that we all carry around with us. His was his lust for power and fame; mine (one of them, anyway) is that I was born in New York. At the French Hospital. In Manhattan.

This is embarrassing. People I thought were friends, men and women I'd known for years, came up and said nasty things like

"I didn't know you were from New York." It did no good at all to explain that my dad was just working there temporarily. It didn't even help to quote the Duke of Wellington, who said about his Irish birth that being born in a stable doesn't make a man a horse. My supposed friends just snickered. I think they're still snickering, behind my back.

It's not fair. I could change my religion or my politics at will. I could, with a little trouble, change my name, or my wife. Even at my age, I could take up a new profession. But I'm stuck for life with my place of birth.

You may find it hard to imagine how awkward, how *shameful*, it is for a semiprofessional Southerner to have been born in the North. And not just in the North, but in the very belly of the beast, in the Big Apple, Noo Yawk itself. For years I have downplayed this fact, going so far as to omit it when filling out forms. Given the chance to write autobiographical squibs I've sometimes resorted to misdirection: "Mr. Reed, a Tennesseean," for instance, or "John Reed grew up in Kingsport, Tennessee." But I thought I'd better tell the FBI the truth. So the White House—my own president that I voted for—outed me. That's right up there for betrayal with having the dictator of Communist Russia to dinner (which came later).

It was some consolation, however, that the appointment gave me a title. When my nomination was confirmed by the Senate, on a slow day, I became "the Honorable" by presidential commission, and I have a piece of paper to prove it. When I start feeling smug about it, humility is easily restored by repeating the mantra "The *Honorable* Edward Kennedy. The *Honorable* Edward Kennedy. . . ." But, still, I've always been a pushover for titles.

Southerners tend to be. Simple Jeffersonian taste might prescribe "sir" or "ma'am" as forms of address in all circumstances save those that call for obscenity, but that has been a lost cause down here ever since planter-plutocrats started appointing each other to high office. One term in the upper house of the state legislature and you're "Senator" for life. A stretch in traffic court makes you "Judge." Any military rank of captain or above—regular, reserve, National Guard, or Civil Air Patrol—can be used without embarrassment until they fire the shots over your grave. This affection for high-sounding forms of address is probably what has led to the widespread misuse of "Reverend." And of course the most honored title of all is "Coach."

Twenty-five years ago I used to tell my students not to call me "Doctor." I told them that form of address should be reserved for physicians, surgeons, dentists, chiropractors, and maybe pharmacists. But this wasn't modesty. No, my secret objection was that "Doctor" isn't grand enough. Any fool can be a doctor and a great many are. (I've been party to creating a few myself.) Any distinction shared with Dr. Robert Mugabe (LL.D., University of Massachusetts) isn't much of a distinction. I prefer the inverse snobbery of the Ivy League's "Mr.," and, in my heart, I really like the Teutonic magnificence of "Professor." It takes, if nothing else, a certain amount of *sitzfleisch* and low animal cunning to get an academic job these days and to hold it long enough to become "Professor."

My buddy Eugene says he never calls anyone "Doctor" who can't deliver a baby and never calls anyone "Professor" who doesn't play piano in a whorehouse. Obviously, I disagree with Eugene on "Professor," and I've even mellowed some on "Doctor." If we restricted that term to what a flack I know calls "vendors in the health-care delivery industry," a lot of high school principals and Presbyterian ministers would get upset. But my opinion of Tom Clancy's history-professor hero in *Patriot Games* dropped considerably when he insisted on that form of address, and I still make fun of my academic colleagues who put "Dr." on their checks.

"The Honorable," though—well, that's different, isn't it? My students can call me "Your Honor," if they want. For that title, it's worth taking an oath to support and defend the Constitution. It may even be worth having people know where I was born. I'm thinking about changing my phone-book listing.

This and That from Here and There

Time for a round-up of regional news that you may have missed. There's no theme to this particular pudding, really, except perhaps the evidence it provides that Southern culture is still kicking, even if in some respects it's on the skids. Let's start with the fact that here in Chapel Hill we have a local band called, well, Southern Culture on the Skids. (Their best song is "Eight-Piece Box.") I ask you: would anyone name a band, say, *New England* Culture on the Skids? I rest my case.

But not all of the musical news these days is so upbeat. A recent marketing study, for instance, reveals that two-thirds of the country-music audience is now female. I have to say that we traditionalists suspected as much.

It seems to me that country used to be a pretty masculine world. Most of the fans were male, and so were most of the singers, old boys who could tear your heart out with a sad song or make you grin with a lyric like "Her daddy calls her 'angel,' and her mama calls her three times a night." It was men who gave us most of the great country titles, like "Because of the Cathouse I'm in the Doghouse with You," "Footprints on the Windshield Upside Down," and, of course, "Take Your Tongue Out of My Mouth (I'm Kissing You Goodbye)." There was always room for a spunky, take-no-crap gal like Loretta ("Don't Come Home A-Drinkin' with Lovin' on Your Mind") Lynn, but most girl singers knew their place and sang songs like "I Want to Be a Cowboy's Sweetheart" or "Stand by Your Man."

But now, it seems, women have quit telling their husbands and boyfriends to change the station, and I think the advent of the music video has something to do with that. It's no accident that homely guys like George Jones, Johnny Paycheck, and Hank Williams Jr. are being replaced by studly hunks whose videos show their pecs. Ironically, this development hasn't been good for female singers. New women singers are coming along, and they'll have careers, but there are fewer Lorettas and Dollys and Tammys these days—Reba McEntire is about the only female superstar—and the megahits are from guys with names like Vince and Garth and Clint. (A friend of a friend recently moved from Siler City, North Carolina, to Nashville and changed his name to "Brick"—watch for him.) It's almost incidental that some of these boys can really sing: others can't, and it hasn't hurt them one bit. "Achy Breaky Heart" has a good beat and Lord knows you can dance to it, but *I* could sing it as well as Billy Ray does.

Speaking of music videos and Nashville, I find it almost touching that officials at David Lipscomb University in Music City banned MTV from television sets in dormitory lounges and the student center,

objecting to both the noise level and the frequently suggestive content.
Hard to believe, isn't it, that these good souls live in the same
world and century as the Netherlanders who (Reuters informs us)
recently wrote a report recommending special fire-safety regulations
for brothels catering to sadomasochists. (I hadn't thought about it,
but obviously it takes longer to escape from a burning building if
you're handcuffed to a bedpost.)

Yes, our world is made up of many diverse and mutually uncom-
prehending communities. It always has been, of course, but these
days they can't simply ignore each other. Forcing disparate cultures
to *notice* one another is the great effect of the modern mass media.
Communications gurus like to argue that the media are making us
look more alike, too, but that's less clearly so. As a recent article on
"territorial television" in the broadcasting trade magazine *Channels*
shows, different folks watch different programs—and region is one
of the differences that makes a difference. *Designing Women*, for
instance, used to be one of the best shows on television (even if it
did get a little preachy sometimes), and it's certainly one of the best
ever set in the South (although that's not saying much). Southerners
seemed to appreciate that: at its peak the program had ratings in
Atlanta and Little Rock nearly half again as high as the national
average. That's about the same regional bonus that *Newhart* and
Murder, She Wrote enjoyed in Burlington, Vermont. Similarly, the
relatively wholesome CBS miniseries *Lonesome Dove* was watched
by 38 percent of all Houston households, but by only 19 percent of
those in New York City, where it was outdrawn by *Full Exposure:
The Sex Tapes Scandal. Miami Vice* got a bigger audience in (no
surprise) Miami. And so forth.

This is nothing new. Twenty-odd years ago the Neilsen ratings
showed only one program *(The Lucy Show)* in the top ten for both
the South and the Northeast, and that was at a time when there were
only three channels for most viewers to choose from. Now that cable
delivers dozens of stations and folks can watch televangelists or pro
wrestlers or soft porn or Spanish-language game shows *twenty-four
hours a day*, it seems to me that the effect of television is likely to
be to allow regional groups, or any others for that matter, to become
even more what they already are. Whether that's good or bad, of
course, depends on what that is.

By the way, researching this subject the other evening, I came across a cable offering called *Glamorous Ladies of Wrestling*, or *GLOW*. I lingered long enough to see the terrorist Palestina, in fatigues and combat boots, treacherously biting the thigh of the California Doll, who sported not one, but two Happy Faces, one on the butt of her Flashdance sweats, the other tattooed on her arm. Hands across the sea . . .

Anyway, the spirit of competition and free enterprise is alive and well here in Dixie. My buddy Hardy tells me there's a guy in Dothan, Alabama, who sells tires for seventy-five cents a pound, and if you can find them cheaper anywhere else he'll give you a goat. I heard a radio ad the other day for a Greensboro used-car dealer who bills himself as a "car-opractor." And my buddy Cliff has even come up with an entrepreneurial solution for the kudzu problem. He proposes to sell it as a pick-your-own crop to Yankee tourists, to put in their terrariums.

Southern businesswomen have sound values, too. A survey by a Chicago executive search firm found that more than 70 percent of female executives in the South opposed federally imposed parental-leave policies, roughly twice the level of opposition found among their peers in the East and West. Despite their manifest good sense, I'm sorry to say that Southern women executives seem to be playing catch-up. A Texas A&M study reported that only 48 percent of Southern male executives had "strongly favorable" attitudes toward women in business, compared to 57 percent in the East and 65 percent in the West. The Midwest trailed the South, though, with only 40 percent strongly favorable.

In other business news, the *Wall Street Journal* reported that Mexican marijuana growers have a "patron saint," Jesus Malverde, a philanthropic drug dealer hanged by the army in 1904. A prayer to him goes:

> Malverde, increase their cravings. If necessary, let the devils help me in this. Let not my healthy countrymen smoke it, at any rate, only the gringos who buy it. Malverde, you light up my path to make harvesting my destiny. You allow me to harvest the grass for the gringo and to make great bunches of silver coins.

(This translation sounds as if it is the work of the Standing Liturgical Commission of the Episcopal Church, but I am assured that it is not.) According to North Carolina agriculture officials, marijuana has long since surpassed tobacco as our state's number one cash crop, but my question is how our guys—good Protestant lads, for the most part—are supposed to compete with this? President Clinton, are you listening?

This and That from Here and There

Here in the Tar Heel State we also grow some collards, and a story in the *Raleigh News and Observer* suggests that some of our folks can eat them, too. It seems that Mr. Mort Hurst from Robersonville consumed seven and a half pounds at one sitting to retain his title as Collard-Eating King. Ole Mort is an eating fool. Earlier he had traveled to Alabama and set a record by inhaling sixteen and a half double-decker Moon Pies in ten minutes. He shared the secrets of his success: (1) three weeks before entering an eating contest he stops smoking, (2) three or four days before the event he calls his friends so they can "brag on him" to the extent that he feels backed into a corner and just has to win, (3) he listens to a record about himself called "The Legend of Ole Eating Mort Hurst," and (4) for the last day he just concentrates on being a big s.o.b. and doesn't speak to anyone, including his wife and children. Incidentally, he doesn't like collards.

Which reminds me, for some reason, of a great country joke I heard a while back:

Q: Why is my finger like a pie?

A: Because it's got meringue on it.

(This requires some familiarity with East Tennessee accents.)

In political news, when the student newspaper at Lander College in Greenwood, South Carolina, asked a number of its readers who the college's next president should be, sophomore Lauri Clements said, "Jefferson Davis—he may be dead, but at least he's Southern." Alas, Lauri, that's no guarantee these days.

In fact, lately I've been taking a lot of flak from Yankee friends about the all-Dixie ticket that now reposes in the White House. That's not fair, of course. I mean, look, we tried to tell you guys about these people. The South has 157 electoral votes and Bill and Al only got

47 of them, mostly from their friends and neighbors in Arkansas and Tennessee. So you Yankees knock it off, OK? The Clinton years are *your* fault.

Seriously, Bill and Al are trouble. Any fool can see some of the bad news coming, but there may be even more. In a few years, for instance, we may have them to blame for an increase in the activity of racist hate groups. Consider this theory about why such activity decreased in the 1980s: "By 1981 the tide had begun to turn [against racist groups]. For one thing, . . . the new administration in Washington's stated aim of reviving America's pride and strength and restoring conservative social and cultural values tended to undermine whatever base of popular support the far right had begun to acquire." Want to guess where that came from? How about from a report called *The Hate Movement Today*, by the Anti-Defamation League. I hope the ADL is wrong (honest)—but I wouldn't bet on it.

On the other hand, some unanticipated consequences of the Clinton presidency may not be all bad. For instance, a lit prof friend of mine thinks it means the end of postmodernism. I didn't follow her reasoning—something to do with words not meaning anything concrete during the Reagan-Bush nightmare—but if she's right, all this may be worth it.

A Sense of Place

Some people—mostly Southerners and geographers—like to argue about how you can tell whether you're in the South. This argument can be more or less serious. My friend Vince Staten, for instance, once ran up a major phone bill calling restaurants on the Interstate to see how far north you can get grits for breakfast. But some heavyweight scholarship has been devoted to the question, too. A Penn State geographer named Wilbur Zelinsky, for example, has compiled some great maps that show where people start painting their barns (roughly the same place where they once began to farm with horses instead of mules, just north of the old National Road through Ohio, Indiana, and Illinois). Zelinsky has also looked to see where creeks stop being called that (or branches, or runs) and become brooks. (If you see the word *brook* in a Southern place-name, you can be sure the real-estate developers have been at work.)

This game can go on and on, and often does. Literally hundreds of criteria have been suggested, from kudzu to sweet ice tea. My own contribution has been to look at phone books to see where people name businesses "Southern" or "Dixie" something-or-other. (Turns out there are a lot of hairdressers named Dixie, but I didn't count them.) My theory, if you can call it that, is that folks outside the South don't do this much.

The phone-book test works remarkably well, which is to say that it confirms my prejudices—like the one that says southern Florida, northern Virginia, and western Texas are only marginally Southern, these days. If it hadn't worked, though, I'd have scrapped the technique and stuck with the prejudices. After all, some of us just *know* when we leave the South.

It seems that, just as some folks are acutely sensitive to light or noise or (they claim) cigarette smoke, some people have a hypertrophied sense of place. Southerners may be especially vulnerable to this inflammation, but it's not just another regional malady, like hookworm or pellagra. For instance, here's an Englishwoman, Jessica Mitford:

> On the train, through Kentucky. There's already a marked change of atmosphere. The women on the train seem to travel in Sears catalogue dreamy date dresses. One is wearing a beige silk sheath, spangled semi-transparent top, high-heeled simulated glass slippers. She's a great kidder. The conductor, checking on reservations, just asked her, "Are you Mrs Jennie Lee Kelley?" She answered, "Can't you see I am, by my browbeaten look?" Shrieks of laughter from all, especially her fat husband . . . Lovely pale green, lush country outside . . . In a Louisville hotel: already the punctuation and spelling are breaking down. A brochure in my room says, "Derby Lounge. Stall's are named and portray famous derby winners. . . ." and also, "YE-OLE KENTUCKIE BREAKFEASTE." Why the hyphen? Borrowed from you-all?

This is exactly the sort of alertness I experience from the minute I get off the plane at Newark. All sorts of everyday things take on special significance when they're *Northern* things. My wife finds this ironic: she says she can move the furniture or get a new hairstyle and I won't notice for months. Maybe so (I haven't noticed), but put me in a new place and by God I *pay attention.*

A while back I wrote that when I used to drive north to college on old U.S. 11, chronic heartburn always set in about Hagerstown, Maryland, and it let up about the same place when I headed south. A book reviewer picked that out as an example of my "characteristic exaggeration," but—as God is my witness—it's the literal truth. What's more, my buddy Jake read the review and wrote to say that the same thing always happened to him somewhere around Newcastle, Delaware.

Jake also sent along a photocopied page from *The Web and the Rock.* As usual, Thomas Wolfe does go on, but he's worth quoting at length:

> George would later remember all the times when he had come out of the South into the North, and always the feeling was the same—an exact, pointed, physical feeling marking the frontiers of his consciousness with a geographic precision. There was a certain tightening in the throat, a kind of dry, hard beating of the pulse, as they came up in the morning toward Virginia; a kind of pressure at the lips, a hot, hard burning in the eye, a wire-taut tension of the nerves, as the brakes slammed on, the train slowed down to take the bridge, and the banks of the Potomac River first appeared. Let them laugh at it who will, let them mock it if they can. It was a feeling sharp and physical as hunger, deep and tightening as fear. It was a geographic division of the spirit that was sharply, physically exact, as if it had been cleanly severed by a sword. When the brakes slammed on and he saw the wide flood of the Potomac River, . . . he drew in hot and hard and sharp upon his breath, there in the middle of the river. He ducked his head a little as if he was passing through a web. He knew that he was leaving South. His hands gripped hard upon the hinges of his knees, his muscles flexed, his teeth clamped tightly, and his jaws were hard. The train rolled over, he was North again.

Hard and sharp and hot and taut—"Every young man from the South has felt this precise and formal geography of the spirit," Wolfe claims, "this tension of the nerves, . . . this gritting of the teeth and hardening of the jaws, this sense of desperate anticipation."

Well, all I feel is indigestion, but the point is that Wolfe gets it right about something physical happening to some of us Southern boys when we leave the South. We're sort of human dowsing rods for Southernness. If you want to map the region, maybe you could just point us north and draw the Rolaid line.

By the way, although I think Jake and I respond (OK, maybe over-respond) to real regional differences, something else was going on with Wolfe's young Southerners. They were reacting not just to real differences—strange accents, strange foods, strange-looking people—but to *expected* ones, expectations nurtured by their own needs and imaginations. "They felt they were invading a foreign country," Wolfe wrote; "they were steeling themselves for conflict [and] looking forward with an almost desperate apprehension to their encounter with the city." ("Desperate anticipation" and "desperate apprehension" in the same paragraph, but that's old Tom for you.) "They were also looking forward to that encounter with exultancy and hope, with fervor, passion, and high aspiration."

"Not me," Jake wrote in the margin. Well, not me, either. But, for a certain sort of dreamy young Southerner, the North—New York City in particular—has always had a special fascination, from afar. Listen to Doug Marlette, the Pulitzer Prize–winning cartoonist who draws "Kudzu." A few years ago, when he moved from Georgia to the Big Apple, Marlette felt obliged to explain himself to his Southern friends and neighbors. "New York's energy, excitement, and vitality have always attracted me," he wrote. "It's the show—the cultural vortex of the race, the storm center of human achievement."

And, he continued, "it holds a special place in the dreamscapes of my youth and the mythic underpinnings of my budding ambition." Marlette recalled how his image of The City came to be:

> As a child growing up in small towns in North Carolina and Mississippi, I visited New York and studied its environs only from television, movies, books, and magazines. The media initiated me into the secrets, mysteries, and allures of the city.
>
> I learned about Macy's from *Miracle on 34th Street*. I knew that Rob and Laura Petrie on the *Dick Van Dyke Show* lived in suburban New Rochelle. The offices of *Mad* magazine were

located on Lexington Avenue. They made fun of ad-men on
Madison Avenue.

Those places and frames of reference were as much a part of
the geographies of my imagination as were Judea and Samaria
from my Sunday school lessons or Vicksburg and Chancel-
lorsville from my history books. And I imbued those alien
landscapes and cultures with a vitality and reality that seemed
achingly absent from my own.

Many young Southerners have felt that way, responding less to
actual places than to their *ideas* of those places—ideas that may be
little more than stereotypes. But there's an irony here. When people
do that, they can help to create the facts they've imagined. New
York's an exciting place, in part, because it's full of young provincials
who have gone there for its excitement.

Incidentally, I don't know what happened, but Doug Marlette
recently moved again, from New York to North Carolina. He's my
neighbor now, just up the road in Hillsborough, and if he has explained that move in print, I haven't seen it. Maybe he feels no
explanation is necessary.

Passing the Bottle

One winter weekend a dozen of us—poets, novelists, and essayists—
gathered in Arkansas to discuss Southern autobiography, and after
the conference was over we went out on the town in Little Rock. It
was my first visit, and, all in all, I'm a little more cheerful now about
having an Arkansas politician running the Big Show. Despite some
accretions of yuppiedom (too many brasseries and bistros to suit me)
Arkansas's capital city is still a pleasantly funky Southern town.

We stayed at a hotel next door to the Old State House, familiar to
television viewers as the scene of Bill Clinton's victory celebration,
and I dropped in to browse in the museum it now houses. In the
museum's newsletter officials were busily pooh-poohing reports in
the national press that the building is haunted by the ghost of a representative killed in an 1837 knife-fight. The knifing death is a matter
of record, but a spokesman protested that "there is no evidence that we
are any more prone to soulless, lifeless zombies than any other state

agency." The alleged sighting of the back of a man dressed in a frock coat, he said, was probably just "a very homely woman in a pantsuit."

That evening we went for supper to Mr. Clinton's favorite Little Rock restaurant, Doe's Eat Place, and pigged out on steak, tamales, and fried shrimp, served family-style at long tables. The beer and wine flowed freely (reminding me of the etymology of the word *symposium*) and the conversation flowed freely, too. When it was my turn, I told one of my favorite stories, which I'd heard at a gathering very much like this one.

It seems there were these two Southern historians who had been to a convention, and after an evening of well-lubricated conversation they dropped into a truck stop for some coffee before retiring. One of them, a little guy who spoke with a lisp (that I undertook to imitate), was talking rather loudly and after a while his friend noticed that the place had fallen silent. Several large, unkempt loungers were listening to him and snickering to each other. They started to make rude remarks, less and less sotto voce, which the speaker didn't seem to notice, but his friend certainly did. "Let's pay up and get out of here before there's trouble," he muttered.

The little guy finally noticed what was going on. To his friend's dismay, he pushed back his chair, stood up, and glared at the locals. "I know what you're thinking," he told them. ("Oh, Lord," his friend thought. "Here we go.") "You think we're pretty sissyfied," he lisped. "*Well.* If *you're* so smart: when did Hank Williams die?" The silence was intense. "January first, nineteen fifty-three. Now shut your goddamn mouths!"

They did.

That story always goes down well with an academic crowd—it shows what a knowledge of history can do for you—and the Little Rock group was no exception. As the laughter died down, however, Our Host, a historian lately diverted into administration, said quietly: "Cityfied."

Say what?

"Cityfied. He said, 'You think we're pretty *cityfied*,' not sissyfied. I was there. That was me—the friend. The other guy was—" and he gave the name. "You got the rest of it right, though."

"Wait a minute," said the Distinguished Male Poet, "I know *him*." And the conversation was off in a different direction. Later, though,

I shook Our Host's hand. It's not often one meets a living legend.

Wiping the grease from our chins, we left Doe's. "You got anything like this in Chapel Hill?" the Celebrated Illustrator asked me. I had to confess that these days we lack the necessary concentration of unselfconscious carnivores to sustain a place like Doe's. "We've got too many folks who are ready to lecture you on how many bushels of corn it takes to produce a pound of meat," I said.

"Yeah," he said. "I'm waiting for them to start on how many bushels it takes for a quart of corn liquor."

We took our symposium on to the bar of the old Capital Hotel, where we talked late into the night. At one point, the conversation turned to the subject of conversation—we had, you might say, a *meta-* conversation. The Expatriate Woman Writer kicked it off by saying how good it was to be back where people *tell stories*. (She teaches in the Midwest.) Someone quoted Roy Reed's characterization of conversation in New York as "hurled stones," compared to the Southern style, "moonshine passed slowly to all who care to lift the bottle." We all nodded sagely and self-satisfiedly, and each took a literal sip.

The Famous Humorist complained gently about his current lady friend, a Yankee, who keeps interrupting his stories, trying to be helpful. I quoted Eudora Welty's character, Miss Edna Earle Ponder, who feared that her dim-witted uncle would encounter some guest at her hotel who "would break in on a story with a set of questions, and wind it up with a list of what Uncle Daniel's faults were: some Yankee." Someone suggested that a nice multicultural gesture would be for Yankees to adopt the Native American "speaking stick," passed from hand to hand. We giggled to think how frustrating that would be for our opposite numbers, professors and writers, in New York.

Yes, the Black New England Poet said, she loved being with other people who answer questions with anecdotes. It was her first time, really, in the South, with Southerners, and she felt as if she had stumbled into a family reunion—of a family she didn't know she had. God bless her.

Later, back in Chapel Hill, I was reminded of her wonderful, generous, unexpected observation as I struggled to write a memorial of my friend Mel Bradford, dead too young at fifty-eight. The first time I met Mel was in a setting very much like the one I've been describing, a gathering of Southern scholars in someone's hotel room.

As it happens, Mel later wrote about a similar evening, and I wound up quoting him. The conversation, he said, involved "the rehearsal of common bonds antecedent to our professional identities, visible as much in the manner of our speaking as in its content—in idiom, in humor, in certain hyperbolic gestures, verging on swagger, panache, and familiarity." He characterized "the round robin of the talk" as "intense and friendly, serious and droll, carried on as if all present feared that it would be some time before they would all be together again and were determined to hear and say it all." All in all, a non-Southern visitor told Mel, it was like—yes!—"a family reunion."

Now, I went to graduate school in New York and I spent a year at Oxford (the one in England), and I can tell you that academic conversation in those parts is stimulating, witty, learned, vicious, all sorts of good things, but no one would ever confuse it with a family reunion. Fortunately, given my occupation, I don't mind cut-and-thrust, but for the long haul—even for eternity—I'll take the Southern mode. "If heaven ain't a lot like Dixie," Hank Williams Jr. sings, "I don't want to go."

Pass the bottle.

II

Southrons, Hear Your Country Call You

Julep Time

Father and General Catchings and Captain McNeilly and Captain
Wat Stone and Mr. Everman would forgather every so often on
our front gallery. These meetings must habitually have taken
place in summer, because I remember Mother would be in
white, looking very pretty, and would immediately set about
making a mint julep for the gentlemen—no hors d'oeuvres,
no sandwiches, no cocktails, just a mint julep. After the first
long swallow—really a slow and noiseless suck, because the
thick crushed ice comes against your teeth and the ice must
be kept out and the liquor let in—Cap Mac would say: "Very
fine, Camille, you make the best julep in the world." She probably did.

Thus William Alexander Percy's memory of his Mississippi boyhood, long ago, from *Lanterns on the Levee*. Many things have
changed, but the heat is still with us. As I write, it is a good deal more
than ninety degrees in the shade, although, to be honest, I'm in an
air-conditioned office, a recourse not available to Percy's parents and
their friends. Still, the mere thought of the steamy heat outside makes
me thirsty. And of course every hot and thirsty Southerner's thoughts
turn to that cooling potation historically associated with Dixieland,
the mint julep. Right?

No, suh.

Twice a year, our Center for the Study of the American South here
in Chapel Hill conducts something called the Southern Focus Poll. We
interview roughly 800 residents of the South and 400 other Americans
about questions of compelling interest to Southerners—or, anyway,
to me. (I should note for the benefit of North Carolina taxpayers that
these questions are not paid for by state funds.) Recently we asked
folks, first, if they'd ever had a julep; second, if they knew what's in
one. Brace yourself.

It turns out only one Southerner in four has ever sipped a julep.
We are, if anything, *less* likely than other Americans to have done
so: 26 percent of us, 29 percent of them. Of course, Southerners are
less likely than Yankees to 'fess up to drinking *anything* alcoholic:
39 percent of us claim to be teetotalers; only 24 percent of non-
Southerners do. This means that Southerners who do drink are slightly

31

more likely than non-Southern drinkers to have drunk juleps—but even most of them haven't.

It's true, of course, that this devilishly delicious concoction isn't a drink for Christians, unless they're Episcopalians, so maybe it's not surprising that among the Wednesday night church-supper crowd (those who go to church more than once a week) four out of five are julep virgins. But so are two-thirds of even those aberrant Southerners who never darken the church door.

Given that the julep has historically been a white man's drink, perhaps it's no surprise that 95 percent of the black Southerners we spoke with had never had one. But neither had 70 percent of the Southern whites.

The julep has also been an aristocrat's drink, sipped in the shade of the veranda by folks like the General and the Captains of Percy's childhood, while the lower orders toiled in the sun, but come on, folks, it's the nineties. This ought to mean that plain folks can drink juleps, too. What seems to be happening instead, though, is that the aristocracy (or what passes for it these days) is drinking wine coolers and lite beer. Only a bare majority (52 percent) even of Southerners with annual incomes over $60,000 have tried the julep.

And the younger generation has no respect for tradition at all. The julep-drinking numbers go like this:

65 or older	39%
45–64	32%
25–44	24%
18–24	9%

But worst of all is the fact that more folks have apparently drunk a julep than know what's in one. Eighty percent of Southerners and 77 percent of non-Southerners said they didn't know; another 10 percent of Southerners and 13 percent of non-Southerners thought they knew, but were wrong. And some of the wrong answers were truly disgusting: 7-Up, creme de menthe, peppermint schnapps, cherries, lemonade, chocolate, orange cream, "juleps," "green stuff," and "a square kind of candy that's chewy." Yuck.

This is a disgrace. I mean, here's a libation that's supposed to be part of the Southern heritage, and most of us don't even know what's in it.

So, listen up, Confederados. I don't care if you never touch the stuff: it's your patriotic duty to know how to make a mint julep. Even *The Mr. Boston Bartender's Guide* has a decent recipe: check it out. Or if that's too much trouble, let Mr. Will Percy tell you how it was done in the old days. Here's how his mother did it:

> Certainly her juleps had nothing in common with those hybrid concoctions one buys in bars the world over under that name. It would have been sacrilege to add lemon, or a slice of orange or of pineapple, or one of those wretched maraschino cherries. First you needed excellent bourbon whisky; rye or Scotch would not do at all. Then you put half an inch of sugar in the bottom of the glass and merely dampened it with water. Next, very quickly—and here was the trick in the procedure—you crushed your ice, actually powdered it, preferably in a towel with a wooden mallet, so quickly that it remained dry, and, slipping two sprigs of fresh mint against the inside of the glass, you crammed the ice in right to the brim, packing it with your hand. Last you filled the glass, which apparently had no room left for anything else, with bourbon, the older the better, and grated a bit of nutmeg on the top. The glass immediately frosted and you settled back in your chair for half an hour of sedate cumulative bliss. Although you stirred the sugar at the bottom, it never all melted, therefore at the end of the half hour there was left a delicious mess of ice and mint and whisky which a small boy was allowed to consume with calm rapture.

That nutmeg must be a Delta thing—I never heard of it anywhere else—but Percy's version is close enough to classic for me. I mean, if you can't trust a Mississippi gentleman to know about juleps, who can you trust? Stick to his instructions and you can't go wrong.

Of course, folks will disagree about some of the details. This is the South we're talking about here, after all. Kentuckians and Virginians will argue about whether to muddle the mint, for instance, and purists will tell you it's not a julep if it's not served in a silver cup. But that's the kind of interstate discord and class snobbery that brought down the Confederacy. As far as I'm concerned, things have reached such a pass these days that you can muddle the mint or not, drink from silver or pewter or a jelly jar if you have to, put nutmeg on it if you must, and crush your ice in a blender if you don't have a wooden mallet or the energy to use it. The important thing is that we not allow the julep to pass from living memory.

Here's to the liberation of our country.

Confederate Agents in the Ivy League

From time to time friends in the North send me clippings and first-hand reports about the progress of Our Nation's cause. I hope my correspondents don't mind, but I've come to think of them as a sort of intelligence service, even something of a Fifth Column. For instance, one expatriate, now a Harvard professor, has sent along a brochure for a Boston bank. Its cover shows a yuppie couple on their boat, sipping wine against a backdrop of the Boston skyline, enjoying the good life that their savings or low-interest loan has made possible. On the bow of the boat, so inconspicuous that it presumably escaped the bank's notice, is a rebel flag decal. My spy labeled the photograph: "The Confederate Navy in Boston Harbor." Keep those cards and letters coming, folks.

Meanwhile, a couple of less cheering reports have come in from the Ivy League—one each, as it happens, from Yale and Harvard.

At Yale, as you may know, there is a residential college named for John C. Calhoun, class of 1804. I've never visited Calhoun College, but it sounds like a sort of oasis in the poststructuralist wasteland of New Haven. In a devil-may-care display of speciesism, for instance, its oak-paneled dining hall is adorned with Old South hunting pictures. "Above the great fireplace at the end of the room," my buddy Alphonse writes, "hangs a portrait of the Great Nullificator with his long white hair brushed defiantly back. His countenance is stern, almost frowning at the rascality of Yankee capitalists." The Fellows' Common Room boasts a framed copy of the *Charleston Mercury*'s announcement of secession, and the college's dean carries the senator's walking stick at commencement, instead of the customary mace. (By the way, where is Preston Brooks's cane when we need it?)

Yale produced nine Confederate generals and a secretary of state, so you might think it only fitting that this aspect of its heritage should be honored. But of course nothing's simple these days. Recently pamphlets appeared, arguing that Yale should change the college's

They suggested by selective quotation not only that Calhoun championed slavery (which he did, of course), but that he championed nothing else. They also pointed out that the sum of his monetary contributions to Yale was one hundred dollars in 1824. (Does this mean that if he'd come across in a bigger way his politics could be overlooked?) To what the college's name should be changed the anonymous pamphlet-writer saieth not, but since all of the Yale colleges are named for dead white men, presumably heterosexual— well, I fear the worst.

Damn it, I think it's time for the loyal remnant at Calhoun College to think about secession. Take the college's emoluments, take its hunting prints and *Charleston Mercury* clipping, take the old man's walking stick, and head south. Maybe it wasn't a good idea to honor Yale with your presence in the first place.

You know, this is the kind of thing that makes otherwise mild-mannered Southern white boys in New England colleges want to chew tobacco, crank up Hank Williams Jr. on the stereo, and run up the rebel flag. Black folks won't believe this, but that last impulse has absolutely nothing to do with them.

Which leads me to the Harvard story. A clipping from the *Boston Globe* tells of the travails of Miss Bridget Kerrigan, a Harvard pre-law student who had the temerity to hang a Confederate battle flag from her dormitory window. The *Globe*'s reporter calls Miss Kerrigan "aggressively Southern," apparently because she wears floral prints and pink sweaters and addresses journalists as "ma'am." In fact, she comes from the Virginia suburbs of D.C., but, as she rightly pointed out, "You can be born in Alaska and still be Southern. It's a state of mind." Besides, her daddy runs a chewing tobacco trade association.

Anyway, soon after Miss Kerrigan's display of Southern pride, the sensitivity police moved in. Her faculty housemasters wrote in an open letter that they "empathize with those for whom public display of the Confederate flag is a source of pain" and rebuked Miss Kerrigan for being "unwilling to join this community spirit by removing her flag." She found herself being Kitty Kelleyed in a Harvard *Crimson* biographical sketch, and the president of the university himself called her action "insensitive" (of course), as well as "unwise" (an argument that doesn't impress Southerners, who, after all, started a war without having any munitions factories).

You know, if the president had really wanted to persuade Miss Kerrigan, he wouldn't have called her insensitive, he'd have criticized her manners. For a well-raised Southerner, that's the killer argument. And, actually, her manners did leave something to be desired. It's true that her flag offended the people she wanted to offend, but it also annoyed some bystanders, including some of her fellow Southerners, black ones in particular.

Jacinda Townsend, of Bowling Green, Kentucky, for instance, responded to Miss Kerrigan's flag by flying one of her own—with a swastika on it. Miss Townsend (who spoke to the *Globe* movingly and eloquently of her own love for the South) said that her intent was to get *all* flags banned, by flying one that she assumed would offend everybody.

Well, it certainly did that, and she finally took it down when the Black Student Association asked her to, saying that it was making black-Jewish relations more difficult. Miss Townsend said that she hadn't realized how monstrously and particularly offensive the swastika is to Jewish students.

Having grown up in the small-town South myself, I believe her. But look here, Miss Townsend, I also believe—in fact, I know—that many white Southerners simply don't realize how threatening you find the Confederate flag. I'm not saying they'd stop displaying it if they *did* realize that (they might just tell you to get over it), but it's a fact that most of them don't mean what you think they mean, any more than you meant what the Jewish students thought you meant.

More about this business of meaning in a minute, but while I'm giving unsolicited advice, I have some for the rebel lass, Miss Kerrigan, too. It comes in the form of a story.

From time immemorial our local chapter of the Kappa Alpha Order has flown the Confederate flag during the week of its Old South Ball. Starting in the 1960s that practice every year occasioned rancorous ill-will, until a few years ago when some genius decided to fly the Confederate national flag, the Stars and Bars proper, instead of the battle flag—whereupon an eerie calm descended. The brothers still honor their traditions, but now with a flag that apparently lacks the offensive connotations of the Southern Cross. Think about that, Miss Kerrigan.

But, of course, one reason nobody objects to the Stars and Bars is that hardly anybody knows what it is. When Yankee Pharisees get going on the unrighteousness of our people and our heritage and you want to stick it in their ear, only the battle flag will do.

Sticking it in their ear is what I take Miss Kerrigan's real purpose to have been, and I respect her for it. Raising hell is a traditional Southern pastime, and she did a bang-up job of it. As she said to the *Globe*, "If they talk about diversity, they're gonna get it. If they talk about tolerance, they better be ready to have it."

In other words, *here's* some "multiculturalism," sucker—in your face.

And what, after all, does the flag mean? To Miss Kerrigan's critics and apparently to the Harvard establishment it means hate, and violence, and the Ku Klux Klan. But to her, she says, it means "all that is noble and young and rebellious and brave. Tenacity in the darkest hour. Respect for truth, integrity, character, and duty. That is the flag of the war for Southern independence."

Who's to say she's wrong about that? Not Jane Tompkins of the Duke English department, who says that "reader-response" critics like herself "deny the existence of objective texts and indeed the possibility of objectivity altogether [thus making discourse] responsible for reality and not merely a reflection of it." Not her colleague Frank Lentricchia, either; what he says of literature—that it "is inherently nothing, or it is inherently a body of rhetorical strategies waiting to be seized"—is surely even more true of colors on a cloth.

So get this: We must establish and maintain a counter-hegemonic discourse. Because the flag is a text that each reader (re)constructs for her/himself, we must foreground its semiotic interrelationship with the historic national liberation struggle of a Third World people, resisting the attempt to valorize or privilege the hegemonic reading. (How'm I doing?)

Buried in this steaming pile of trendy b.s. is a valid point, which is that since 1865 rebellious spirits of many nations have seen the Confederate flag as a symbol of freedom. Many have seen the Southern cause as the cause of liberty—tragically flawed by its link to human bondage, sure, but the Confederates paid the price for that.

You don't believe me? Read the account in Darden Pyron's biography of Margaret Mitchell of how *Gone with the Wind* was received. It was read around campfires on both sides of the Spanish Civil War; each side, believing its cause was just, identified with the Confederates. Later, the book was popular among the anti-Nazi resistance, then within the captive nations of Eastern Europe.

I can attest to that last audience. On my office wall is a news photo from Erfurt, formerly of the German Democratic Republic, shortly after its liberation. It shows Chancellor Kohl speaking to a large crowd in the town square. Many of his listeners wave West German flags. Far in the back, however, one citizen is waving the battle flag of the late C.S.A.

And I can top even that. For a while a few years ago I had a folded Confederate flag on my office desk. It was there because an Israeli friend had written to say that his eighteen-year-old son, a tank gunner in the Israeli army, had been reading about Nathan Bedford Forrest and wanted a rebel flag to fly from his turret. You'd be surprised how hard it is to find a Confederate flag in Chapel Hill these days, but when I put out a call for help, I got *two*: one from a Kappa Alpha I know, the other from a friend who happened to be passing Stuckey's on the Interstate. I sent one on to the Golan Heights, where it flies today (I have a photograph). I put the redundant flag on my messy desk.

One day I had a visitor, a scholar from Tblisi, in then-Soviet Georgia, on an American tour. He saw the flag on my desk, recognized it, and asked where he could get one. Naturally, I insisted that he take mine. Now, I don't know if he really understood what he was saying, but after he thanked me he said (and I swear this is true), "Someday this will fly in a free Georgia."

Capture the Flag

My buddy Chris has written with some suggestions for the upcoming Atlanta Olympics. For starters, he thinks it's only right that Atlanta fly the Stars and Bars, as well as Old Glory. Chris observes that the Catalans got to fly their flag in Barcelona, and personally I like the idea of the South as a sort of American Catalonia, so my first impulse is to unleash a rebel yell for that proposition. But let's think about it a bit before we write the organizing committee.

We Southerners have a problem that the Catalans don't. Unlike their historic symbols, which are signs of national unity, the symbols

of the Confederacy these days signify and inspire mostly discord.
Witness the fact that many of Georgia's and virtually all of Atlanta's
political bigshots are now campaigning to end what the *Atlanta Jour-*
nal-Constitution calls the "disgrace" of including the Confederate

battle flag as part of the Georgia state flag. Far from wanting to fly
the rebel flag at the Olympics, these folks want it completely out
of sight before the television cameras come to the City Too Busy to
Hate and beam it out worldwide. The *Journal-Constitution*'s editorial
cartoonist even did a scurrilous little number juxtaposing the Nazi flag
flying over the 1936 Olympics and the Southern Cross waving over
the 1996 Games. (The cartoonist, a young man from Seattle, claims
he got some death threats, but not nearly enough to suit me.)

All the arguments for and against changing have been aired at
length in the Georgia press, and they even spilled over to the editorial
page of *USA Today*, which gratuitously urged Georgia to rejoin the
Union, then printed the predictable letters. Most of the pros and cons
you can probably reconstruct for yourself, and I won't rehash them
here. One complication in the Georgia case, however, is that the
present flag was adopted only in 1956—to symbolize resistance to
desegregation, its opponents claim. Its defenders find in the record of
the legislative deliberations no signs of that motive and a good many
indications that the point was to honor the Confederacy in light of
the upcoming Civil War centennial. But those who object to honoring
the Confederacy, of course, don't see that as an improvement.

Another factor that gives the Georgia dispute a special twist is the
wannabe nature of Atlanta. I mean, this is a town whose Convention and Visitors Bureau hired an out-of-state PR firm to devise a
slogan for it. Predictably, it came up with something utterly insipid:
"Atlanta—Hometown to the World." Shoot, my buddy Martin did
better off the top of his head: "Atlanta—The South Stops Here." My
personal favorite is "Atlanta: Not Bad for Georgia," but Atlanta's too
insecure to go in for sly self-deprecation. It's the kind of place where
you get off an airplane and confront a sign that says "Welcome to Atlanta: A World-Class, Major League City." (Really. Try substituting
London or Tokyo—or even Los Angeles or Budapest—to see how
pitiful that line is.)

Anyway, getting back to the flag, it seems that most white Georgians don't share their betters' distaste for the flag of their ancestors.

A Mason-Dixon Poll, for instance, showed that 66 percent of all Georgians wanted to keep the present flag and only 29 percent wanted to scrap it. Even a majority of black Georgians said the current flag was all right with them. Given this, and the fact that Atlanta still doesn't muster a majority in the Georgia legislature, it seems certain that the flag will be retained. But one Atlanta pol told me at supper one night that if he and his friends can't get it changed back to what it was before 1956 they simply won't fly it. (He didn't know, of course, and apparently hardly anyone else does either, that the old Georgia flag is actually just the Stars and Bars, the Confederate national flag, with the state seal—motto: "Wisdom, justice, moderation"—substituted for the stars. It was adopted in 1879 with the restoration of home rule after Reconstruction.)

Now, when these conflicts arise, my first reaction—and surely that of many sensible people—is always to wonder whether our politicians and journalists don't have something better to do. After all, it's not as if Alabama and Georgia and North Carolina don't have some real problems, even a few real problems of race relations. I feel like "Soapy Sam" Wilberforce, nineteenth-century bishop of Oxford, confronted with a bitter controversy over whether priests could wear chasubles. "What a plague it is," His Lordship complained, "that people cannot have common sense as well as earnestness."

But like the chasuble question, this *is* important, not in itself, but in the matter of what it stands for. The Confederate flag is as offensive to some of our fellow citizens as Romish vestments were to some of Wilberforce's, and in many of the same ways. Like their Victorian counterparts, our latter-day Roundheads see scraps of colored cloth as representing doctrines they find repugnant, doctrines once thought to have been extirpated for all time. Those of a more Whiggish disposition, like Atlanta's leaders, see the flag as an emblem of opposition to progress and enlightenment. The flag's partisans, meanwhile, refuse to accept their adversaries' definition of what it is they are defending. And, God knows, everybody is earnest.

Can we sort this out? Is there anything helpful to be said, or must this all just come down to a political contest of wills?

First of all, let's stipulate that it's nobody's business but Georgians' *what* goes on their flag. *USA Today* may not have the sense to stay out of this affair, but Southerners, at least, should recognize that states' rights is one thing the Southern Cross stands for, and if a state can't even choose its own flag maybe it's time to think about giving secession another try.

But on the larger question of what an appropriate symbol of Southern unity might be, I do feel entitled to some opinions, and in fact I have two: first, that the South needs and deserves *some* sort of symbols; second, that the Confederate flag won't do anymore.

Let me tell a story. Some time back a friend sent me an issue of the *Jaguar Journal*, a student publication of the Falls Church, Virginia, high school. It contained a rather lame attack on the Confederate flag as a symbol of slavery and oppression, paired with an eloquent defense by a young woman named Wendi Crouch, who quoted the country-music group Alabama: "And we were leaning, leaning on / The everlasting arms of love, / Livin' all the simple joys / This Dixie boy is made of." A survey revealed that nearly half of the school's multiracial, multicultural student body felt that there was nothing wrong with displaying the flag under almost any circumstances; as one student put it, the flag is a "symbol of everything the South stands for: unity and pride." Another third of the school's students felt that the flag shouldn't be flown officially (for instance, over state capitols). Only one student in six felt that display of the flag should be banned altogether.

Now, I've said many snide things in my time about northern, or "Occupied," Virginia, and maybe I've been too harsh. Notice, however, that the students' defense of the flag was not on the grounds of its association with the Confederacy. Those who spoke for the record valued it as an emblem of Southern pride *in the present.*

That pride is considerable. At the William and Mary commencement a couple of years ago a student speaker shared with the audience what his father had told him as he began his freshman year: "Remember what you come from," his daddy had said. "You're a Virginian and a Southerner." (My informant was reminded of his own father's parting words, thirty years ago: "Well, son, you'll meet all kinds up here.") Southerners feel themselves to be citizens of no mean city, and if the Confederate flag is the only symbol of our community available, we'll use it—one reason many who don't care much about the Confederacy one way or the other are attached to its flag.

It is, however, simply a fact that fewer self-identified Southerners each year feel any attachment to the Confederate heritage. In the first place, a steadily increasing proportion either don't know or don't care what their ancestors' sympathies were. Thirty-seven percent of the white respondents to a 1992 Southern Focus Poll didn't know whether they had family who fought in the Late Unpleasantness, and another 30 percent said they knew they didn't. Of the remaining third, one in six had only Union ancestors and a quarter had kinfolk on both sides. In other words, something under 20 percent of today's white Southerners have an exclusively Confederate heritage, and know it, and both ignorance and mixed ancestry are more common among younger Southerners than among older ones.

In addition, fewer and fewer self-identified Southerners are native whites to begin with. Both Asian- and Hispanic-Southerners are more common each year: I know plenty of each. A good many migrants from Yankeedom are quite ready to sign up, if we'll let them. And surveys show that most Southern blacks now identify themselves as Southerners—a welcome development, in my view. But you can't expect most of these folks to be attached to the Confederate flag. In particular, the flag divides Southerners on racial lines. Asked by the *Atlanta Journal-Constitution* whether the flag is more a symbol of racial conflict or of Southern pride, Southern whites picked regional pride 76 percent to 17 percent, while blacks saw racial conflict 58 percent to 31 percent. (Blacks were far more tolerant of the song "Dixie," seeing it as a symbol of Southern pride by a margin of 48 percent to 40 percent.)

Given all this, it seems to me that trying to make all true Southerners salute the Confederate flag excludes altogether too many people who have a right to the label and who could be valuable recruits to the cause. On grounds of both prudence and doing the right thing, there's much to be said for finding or devising other symbols of regional identity, more inclusive ones that can be saluted by anyone of goodwill.

And here we can learn from the Catalans. In their view anyone who moves to their region and adopts their ways (in particular, their language) is Catalan. Period. This means they don't face the problem that Southerners now face, that of being a minority in much of their own land. Migration to Catalonia contributes to the nation's economic and political strength, offsetting its relatively low birthrate without undermining its unity.

And if we give up pretending that the Confederate flag has a claim on the loyalty of all Southerners—well, then, of course state governments ought to take it off their flags. (I'm not wild about some of the company that conclusion puts me in, but it seems inescapable.) Let those who honor the Confederate heritage do so privately.

But let's not go overboard. The symbols of the Confederacy shouldn't be denied to those who are entitled to them and moved by them. Sixty-odd years ago, Allen Tate complained about "well meaning orators" who told white Southerners "that they need not be ashamed of a grandfather who fought with Lee, that the grandfather could not have known how God had to use four years of war to show them the righteousness of Big Business and the iniquity of the farm." But more has changed since 1930 than the *New Republic* (in which Tate wrote): I can't recall the last time I heard someone telling white Southerners that. Indeed, those whose grandfathers fought with Lee must often feel these days that they *are* being asked to apologize for their heritage, if not to renounce it altogether. As the Marxist historian Eugene Genovese observed during an exchange on this subject at a recent meeting of the American Studies Association, no one should be required to spit on his ancestors' graves. We should all wish the latter-day Confederates luck in rescuing their symbols from the racist trash who have lately sought to appropriate them.

Flagging Energy

We have it on good authority that the peacemakers are blessed, and that's only fair, because we sure catch hell in this world. Not long ago I suggested that most Southerners who display the Confederate flag are not bigots, and got some hate mail to the effect that only a bigot could believe that. Then I observed that there's something to be said for state symbols less divisive than that same flag, whereupon I found myself being chastised by folks who apparently believe that *that* is not a matter on which decent people can disagree. Political correctness comes in a variety of flavors, doesn't it?

Anyway, I'm now in a position to compare the two sorts of enthusiasts. I could even say the whole exercise was just an experiment to let me make that comparison, but that wouldn't be true. (Incidentally, if you think you're tired of reading about the rebel flag, think how tired I am of writing about it. And you can just turn the page. I have to stay here and get through to the end of this somehow.)

My major observation is that the flag's defenders have better manners than its opponents. They avoided ad hominem arguments and guilt-by-association, and (this is interesting) they wrote to me personally instead of to my editor. Their tone was usually more one of sorrow than of anger—although that may just have been recognition of the fact that I'd pretty obviously like to be able to agree with them. On the other hand, say this for the reformers who complained: at least they understood what I was saying. The traditionalists wasted a lot of shot on arguments I never made and don't accept.

Since they took the trouble to write, and since they were so nice about it, let me rephrase my argument in terms that they may find more agreeable. Try this: have you ever considered that maybe modern Georgia doesn't *deserve* the Confederate flag?

Look, we're going to be hearing a lot more about this flag business. So far the Georgia flap has received the most attention, partly because of the Olympic tie-in, partly (I suspect) because most of the national press has regional bureaus in Atlanta. But you may also have heard that next door in Alabama the flag's opponents recently went to court to get an order forbidding the state to fly it over the capitol where Jefferson Davis took his oath of office. In Mississippi, on Martin Luther King Jr.'s birthday in 1993, Aaron Henry told an audience at Mississippi College that if King were alive today, changing the state flag would be one of his top three priorities. (I forget the other two.) Obviously the winds of change are just starting to blow.

Incidentally, Mississippi put the Southern Cross on its state flag in 1894, long before Georgia, not hesitating to resort to the kind of subterfuge that would later give literacy tests a bad name. Here's part of the description: "It [the state flag] incorporates the national colors and has 13 stars of the original colonies. It has a union square with a ground of red and a broad blue saltier thereon, broadened with white and emblazoned with stars." Just coincidence, we are to suppose, that the result happens to be the Confederate battle flag.

Anyway, Ernest Renan once observed that the existence of a nation requires that some things be forgotten, and he was obviously right about that, as we're seeing in the break-up of alleged nations around the world today. But the Southern nation somehow has to surmount two facts: (1) Southerners won't forget any time soon what the Confederate flag means to them, and (2) unfortunately it means different things to different Southerners. As I say, the South must surmount these facts—that is, if it's to have a future as well as a past.

There have been some studies of what the flag means. All show that to most Southern whites it means one of two things. For some, like my most recent correspondents, it conjures up a variety of worthy Memorial Day sentiments having to do with tradition, duty, honor, valor, sacrifice, and so forth. For a growing number of others, less historically minded, the flag's specifically Confederate associations are muted. For them it connotes simply a hell-raising, good-timing, outlaw kind of Southern pride. The songs of Hank Williams Jr., for instance, often "brag on that rebel flag" and his fans wave it at his concerts, but he doesn't mean any harm by it and they don't either. (It's a white Southern thing. You wouldn't understand.)

Now, if you expect either group—the filiopietistic or the boogie-till-you-puke—to renounce or abandon its orientation, you've got a long wait coming. But neither of these views is shared or even understood by most non-Southerners or, more importantly, by most Southern blacks. The same studies show that most black Southerners (and a small minority of white ones) see the flag as a sign of the Ku Klux Klan or, more generally, of resistance to the civil rights movement. And, of course, they're not always wrong about that.

Recently I paid a visit to the new civil rights museum in Memphis. Located in the old Lorraine Motel, where Martin Luther King was shot, this has to be the world's *wordiest* museum—wall after wall of text to read. I was skimming my way through the place when I came across a quotation from James Jackson Kilpatrick, back when he was still a Richmond newspaperman and no friend of desegregation. Kilpatrick wrote then that he was taken aback by the sight of a flag once carried into battle by brave and honorable men, being waved by a hateful rabble who turned out to bully black schoolchildren. It gives one pause, he wrote.

It still should, because that association is not merely a leftover, an artifact of the 1950s and 1960s. There's no mistaking the meaning of the rather grim householder in my hometown who flies the battle flag once a year—on Martin Luther King's birthday. When the Klan sent a few dozen outside agitators to march down Chapel Hill's main street a few years ago, they carried that flag. And ads for biker regalia in *Easy Rider* magazine sometimes offer the choice of the swastika or . . . that flag.

The jackals who deploy the flag this way are in a perverse collaboration with the flag's opponents to make the symbols of the Confederacy stand for white supremacy and nothing else. Those who want to defend the flag might give some thought to defending it against *them*. A while back I read a news item from Montgomery reporting that a racist skinhead group had announced its intention to decorate Confederate graves. The usual crowd of anti-racist groups turned out to protest the skinheads' very existence, but my question was: where were the Sons of Confederate Veterans? I wish that they, too, had turned out—to protest this desecration.

We need more stories like that, and like one from Roanoke reporting that the SCV there joined with the city's black mayor and its oldest black Presbyterian church to celebrate the anniversary of the installation of a stained-glass window honoring Stonewall Jackson. The window was installed by an early minister whose parents had attended a Sunday school for slaves, established by Jackson when he was a professor at VMI. *That*'s the kind of story that shakes up preconceptions, that suggests history's not as simple as the textbooks paint it.

I hope it's not too late to redeem the Old Flag, but it will certainly take a mighty effort, which has to start with some recognition of what it now means to many of our fellow citizens. Meanwhile, attempts to universalize the Confederacy's symbols (by including them in state flags, for instance) imply either that those symbols are black folks', too, or that black folks don't count.

Given that, shouldn't the flag's partisans—those of goodwill—say something to their opponents like this:

(1) We don't accept your interpretation of what the flag means, and if we feel like it, we'll fly it, put it on our cars, tattoo

it on our foreheads, whatever we damn well please—meaning by it what we mean by it, not what you think we mean.

(2) However, we understand that it does mean something different to you.

(3) We also recognize that there's no more chance that you'll buy our interpretation than that we'll buy yours.

(4) Symbols of the South (a fortiori, a state flag) should enlist the loyalty and affection of as many Southerners (citizens of the state) as practicable. (In other words, if anything should require a concurrent majority, this is it.)

(5) Therefore, we're willing to look for symbols of the South (a state flag) we can all be attached to.

That strikes me as a coherent and reasonable position, and I'd be very curious to know which part of it my critics don't accept.

Of course, that just gets us to the hard part. What kinds of symbols fill that bill? If you simply *make up* something, you're likely to wind up with synthetic pseudo-tradition, like Kwanzaa, or, if you're really inept, something like the Atlanta Olympics' Whatizit, a semiotic black hole that not only has no meaning itself but drains the meaning out of everything in its vicinity. When *Southern* magazine went looking for regional symbols a few years ago, it ran into this problem. Its suggestions were so sterile, so unevocative, that I can't even remember what they were.

With time, though, constructed symbols take on meaning (OK, maybe Whatizit's an exception). Every flag was new once: no one had died for it. You have to start somewhere. What could be a suitable emblem of Southern unity?

Personally, I'm partial to one of those dancing pigs you see on barbecue signs. No, seriously: a good barbecue joint may be the one place you'll find Southerners of all descriptions—yuppies, hippies, and cowboys, Christians and sinners, black and white together. Not dignified enough for you? Well, lack of *that* concern is a regional tradition, too. Remember how "Dixie" goes on about "buckwheat cakes and Injun batter" that "makes you fat and a little fatter"? Elvis could get with that. Oprah, too. And Delta Burke. Maynard Jackson. Bill Clinton.

But if an anthropomorphic pig just won't do as a symbol for the new, aerobic South—Dixie Lite—I've got two examples of something a little more cerebral. The first is the strange case of the Southern Students Organizing Committee, a group that sixties trivia buffs may recall as a sort of regional affiliate of the Students for a Democratic Society. Its members delighted in mixed messages: their newsletter was called *The Rebel Yell* and their logo was two clasped hands, black and white, superimposed on the battle flag. As I heard it, their SDS comrades from the Northeast and West Coast found all this about as amusing as the Klan must have, just couldn't handle it, and drummed SSOC out of the Movement. I'll forgive SSOC a lot for that.

Just so, last year I was startled, then amused, then heartened to see the battle flag flying from a student residence at the College of Charleston—right next to the green, red, and black banner of black nationalism. I have no idea who flew those flags together, or why, but that sort of juxtaposition can make people stop and think, and I'm optimist enough to believe that's usually not a bad thing.

These examples make me wonder whether there's some way to universalize the Confederate symbols after all, some way to accept the past for what it was, not deny it or forget it, but transform it for our common use. Some other people have been thinking along these same lines lately, and maybe—just maybe—they're getting somewhere. Consider, for instance, the T-shirt designed by *Southern Reader*, a quirky, neo-secessionist, "eco-regionalist" bimonthly out of Oxford, Mississippi. It bears a battle flag, transformed: black and white on a field of green. And a motto from James Brown: "Keep It Funky." I don't know about you, but I think it would be delightful if a few thousand spectators turned up at the Atlanta Olympics in those shirts. If nothing else, it would drive the network guys crazy.

Mississippi Musing

Back in Black History Month, 1993, a *USA Today* story on Afro-American historical sites mentioned a "Black Confederate Memorial" in Canton, Mississippi: a "20-foot obelisk . . . built in 1894 to honor Harvey's Scouts, one of the black units that operated behind Union lines to harass supply shipments." As it happened, I read that story while spending some time in Jackson, twenty miles or so south of Canton. Visions of a lucrative screenplay dancing in my head, I set out through a chilly February rain to find the monument.

Canton turned out to be a pleasant county seat that Sherman somehow neglected to burn (unlike Jackson, which was known as "Chimneyville" when old Cump got through with it). I drove past a charming little Episcopal church and several imposing houses from the days of King Cotton to the classic courthouse square, where I asked a number of citizens, black and white, where their nationally advertised monument could be found. None of them knew anything about it. Finally, a lady in a gift shop on the square thought she might know what I was looking for (at least she knew what an "obelisk" is), and I followed her directions to the edge of town. Sure enough, there it was, surrounded by a cast iron railing. I got out and trudged through the drizzle for a closer look.

The inscriptions on the base were worn almost to illegibility, and I had to smear them with some cold mud before I could read the words. The first was straightforward enough ("Loyal Faithful True / Were Each and All of Them"), but the next read, "Erected by W. H. Howcott to the Memory of the Good and Loyal Servants Who Followed the Fortunes of Harvey Scouts During the Civil War." Hmmm. Did *USA Today* get it wrong? Surely not. But the last inscription clinched it. "A Tribute to My Faithful Servant and Friend, Willis Howcott," it said. "A Colored Boy of Rare Loyalty and Faithfulness, Whose Memory I Cherish With Deep Gratitude. / W. H. Howcott." So much for my screenplay. It would have been a hard sell, anyway.

There are lessons here that the rest of my time in Mississippi only served to confirm, beginning with the fact that you shouldn't believe everything you hear or read about the place. Another lesson is that history is close to the surface there, but, like those inscriptions, it's not always easy to read, and once you've made it out it's not always clear what it means.

One Sunday, I drove the forty-five minutes to Vicksburg. Touring the siege lines in my rented Geo Metro, half-remembered poems by Allen Tate and James Dickey floating in my head, I mused as I often do on the sheer unrecoverable *otherness* of the past. (Not for me, I'm afraid, Faulkner's famous line about its not being dead, not even past.) Surrounded by visiting Boy Scouts and Midwesterners in Winnebagos, I found it almost impossible to reconstruct the noise and the heat, the smoke and blood, much less the sentiments and emotions that drove those men. And here the Park Service's otherwise excellent maps and taped commentary were no help at all.

Amid the grandiose monuments erected by various Northern states to their veterans I almost missed the modest marker for a West Virginia unit. West-by-God-Virginia. What prompted those mountain boys to come all this way to fight, and some of them to die, in the sweltering heat of a Mississippi summer? I doubt that the sentiments of Julia Ward Howe's pious battle hymn had much to do with it. Hatred for the haughty lowlanders I could believe—hanging Jeff Davis from a sour apple tree—or even just the adventure of it, and once you've begun it's hard to quit. But how about the good and loyal servants of the Harvey Scouts? What could have been in *their* minds, as they helped their masters fight the blue-belly invaders? Could it have been as simple as the friendship Mr. Howcott claims? Even Howcott himself: When he put up his imposing monument to Willis and the others, whom did he want to impress? His neighbors? The Yankees of 1894? Us? How could we ever hope to know?

Of the hundreds of monuments that litter the park at Vicksburg, my favorite is Missouri's. That state had sons on both sides, and the monument honors them all. At one point hostile Missouri units faced each other across a scant few yards of no-man's land. During a cease-fire, the Park Service tape informs us, an officer of the Confederate unit visited his Union counterpart across the lines. As he was leaving, the Union officer expressed the hope that they would meet again, in a restored Union. "The only union I hope to share with you, sir," his fellow Missourian replied, "is in the Hereafter."

It's interesting to see how the park's tape and brochures and videos and monuments treat the Confederates. In general, they cleave to what I've come to think of as the Old Settlement, the consensus that obtained from the 1890s until quite recently. They treat the war's outcome as providential (this is the federal Park Service, after all), but the Confederates are granted their valor and honor and good faith. That tacit agreement is certainly under attack these days in venues other than Civil War battlefield parks, and I wonder how much longer it will last even there.

But if interpretations change, some inconvenient facts will still remain, to keep us honest. As we think about what that war was about, and why men fought (not exactly the same question), we need to remember not only the Southerners in the Union Army but also "Northern men of Southern principles" like General Pemberton, the Confederate commander at Vicksburg, a Pennsylvanian. And there's that obelisk in Canton, whatever it means. Things are never as simple as we might like them to be.

Moving on to the town of Vicksburg itself, I surveyed the remains of that once-bustling riverport, among them many fine houses now turned into bed and breakfast establishments. The big news locally was that riverboat gambling had recently been approved, which everyone seemed to expect would revitalize the local economy. A number of other Mississippi River and Gulf Coast towns already have floating casinos, and so far the economic bonanza seems to be real enough. I don't entirely understand, however, why this Baptist-Methodist state has suddenly become so enthusiastic for this one kind of gambling. It must be something like Harry Golden's scheme for "vertical integration." Golden noticed that Southern whites insisted on segregation only for activities that involved blacks and whites sitting together, so he proposed taking the seats out of restaurants, schools, and buses. Just so, gambling seems to be OK in Mississippi only if you're afloat. (My favorite example is the Splash Casino, on a boat moored in some sort of bog in landlocked Tunica County, where the managers now have a problem because the water level is falling. I picture guys with garden hoses trying to get it back up before the state inspector arrives with his dipstick.)

Anyway, no visitor to Vicksburg should miss the curious little museum in the old courthouse building. A half-dozen cluttered rooms display relics of the native Indians and of prominent local families, mementoes of the cave-dwelling days during the siege, Coca-Cola memorabilia (the first Coke was supposedly bottled in Vicksburg), the Louisiana banknote with the word "Dix" (by one theory the origins of the word *Dixieland*), photographs of steamboat races and famous roustabouts, and literally hundreds of other souvenirs of Vicksburg life. I was reminded by this delightful omnium gatherum of Shane Leslie's description of the museum in Reading at the turn of the century: a relic looted from a nearby abbey at the Reformation was displayed in a glass case, labeled "Hand of Saint James."

When my wife came to visit, I took her back to Vicksburg, and we had Sunday dinner at a restaurant high on a bluff over the Mississippi, next to one of the Confederate artillery emplacements that had failed to keep the Yankee gunboats from slipping past in the dark of one fateful night. Below us, the Interstate spanned the great river now, carrying eighteen-wheelers and tourists west to Texas and beyond, and the river traffic was confined to barges. As we were leaving, I noticed among the signed pictures of celebrities in the foyer one of Alex Haley—another Southerner who tried to make the past speak and who (it now appears) finally had to put words in its mouth.

The New America

Yeah, I know we've got two Southerners in the White House. Don't rub it in, OK? As Miss Scarlett used to say, I'll think about it tomorrow. Let's talk about sports.

As you probably know, in four years jocks and TV cameramen from around the world will converge on Dixie for the next Olympic Games. Atlanta beat out Athens (the one in Greece) for the privilege of playing host in 1996, a victory all the sweeter because that year will mark the 100th anniversary of the modern Games. Georgia in July is not where I would choose to exert myself, but I guess the folks who make the decision aren't the same ones who do the exerting. Anyway, those of us who enjoy secondary sweat will be seeing a lot of it.

We'll also be seeing a lot of Atlanta, which is pretty much the point as far as the boosters are concerned. Years ago, W. J. Cash wrote about the skyscrapers going up in Southern towns, which had "little more use for them than a hog has for a morning coat," that these buildings were erected just for the glory of it, another "native gesture of an incurably romantic people, enamored before all else of the magnificent and the spectacular." That observation helped me understand the Knoxville and New Orleans World's Fairs, financial catastrophes but nevertheless successes, and it helps explain Atlanta's obsession with the Olympics, too. Besides, Scarlett's hometown and this quadrennial festival of commercialism and jingoism were made for each other.

On the bright side, there's no question that the Barcelona Olympics were great for the morale of Catalonia, and the 1996 Games could be equally bracing for the South. My buddy Chris was impressed, for instance, by how the International Olympic Committee was bullied into using Catalan as one of the official languages at Barcelona. "The sports commentators," he wrote me, "mindlessly reading what they were handed, told us that 'Catalan is not a dialect of Castilian,' which is technically correct. Similarly, Southern English is not a dialect of Nebraskan." Chris wants to start a campaign for both Yankee and Southern English announcements in Atlanta, and I think that's a splendid idea. It would be deeply satisfying to hear "The javelin competition will begin momentarily" also rendered as "The spear-chuckin' contest is fixin' to commence directly." You all want to form a national committee?

Anyway, seriously, the Atlanta Games could be very good for the South. But that's not the way they're shaping up. As it happens, I was in Atlanta just after the Olympics, when Atlantans were all agog about what they'd let themselves in for. At supper one night I listened to Michael Lomax, the personable chairman of the Fulton County Board of Commissioners, who had just returned from Barcelona and was talking about how Atlanta is going to do it better. What he had to say was troubling. Although Barcelona managed to present itself as both an emerging world city and the proud capital of a proud region with a distinguished history and culture, it sounds as if Atlanta is fixing to pretend that it's not a Southern city at all. When a couple of us objected that Atlanta's plans seemed to be ignoring the city's history and regional context, Lomax cheerfully agreed. Atlanta has been the capital of the New South for the last hundred years, he said, and it's time to move on. "We plan to present Atlanta as the New America." Now, *that's* a scary thought. Take away its history and its status as the South's de facto capital and the only thing remarkable about Atlanta is the number and variety of its table-dancing establishments.

But I do understand the impulse. In the first place, Catalonia can afford to be proud: it's pretty much carrying the rest of Spain economically. The South, though, is still to some degree a colonial dependency. Emphasizing our cultural distinctiveness and separatist history could be bad for business, discouraging outside investment— and nowhere does that argument carry more weight than in Atlanta.

Moreover, like Michael Lomax, most members of Atlanta's political elite these days are black. When V. S. Naipaul toured the South not long ago, he was struck by black Southerners' almost willful lack of interest in their own and their region's history, and although Naipaul may not have met a representative sample, his observations certainly apply to Lomax and his colleagues. But this is the first post-segregation generation, and like first-generation immigrants elsewhere in the United States they may prefer to emphasize their American future, not a past that they find painful. Personally I'd rather they forget it ("move on," as Lomax put it) than dwell exclusively on their historical grievances, but I hope those aren't the only choices.

In any case, just because I understand what Atlanta's doing doesn't mean I *like* it. As my friend David Moltke-Hansen is fond of saying, the South is a region with more than a future, and I'm happy to say that ignoring Atlanta's heritage may be easier said than done. Several events have been scheduled for nearby Stone Mountain, for instance, and Lomax acknowledges that that's going to be a problem. It'll be easy enough to get rid of the hoop-skirted hostesses, but the visages carved on the Mount Rushmore of the Confederacy will be a little harder to obscure, and if the television cameras don't linger on those figures it will be a triumph for Atlanta's PR people. (Alas, we can probably also count on announcers' informing us that it was on Stone Mountain that the founding of the second Ku Klux Klan was marked with a giant flaming cross, a fact few Atlantans, nostalgic or otherwise, want to dwell on, and I'm with them there.)

A taste of what we can expect from Official Atlanta in the next four years was given to viewers of the Barcelona Games' closing ceremonies when the city unveiled the mascot for the 1996 Games, a blue, computer-designed noid with tennis shoes and lightning-flash eyebrows, called "the Whatizit." (Incidentally, the dancer inside the Whatizit turns out to be a graduate of my university, a former head cheerleader—in case you wondered what cheerleaders do when they grow up.) Even the thing's name speaks to the city's loss of identity, and its form—well, one Atlantan described it as just "a goddamn comma," but at least five others took pleasure in telling me that it looks like nothing so much as a spermatozoon. (Its race is indeterminate, but we may hear demands for equal time for ova.)

Come to think of it, though, this spermiform critter may be appropriate in a way: Michael Lomax told me that 120,000 condoms were distributed at Barcelona's Olympic Village, and the Dream Team wasn't even staying there. (He joked about the opportunities for commercial tie-ins. Atlanta humor.) I also read in the paper that visiting Atlantans were impressed by the absence of bikini tops on Spanish beaches and by Barcelona's popular coed bathroom with see-through walls. Where's Franco when you need him?

Anyway, even some non-Establishment Atlantans aren't wild about the Whatizit. The city's alternative newspaper found one young woman who liked it ("It's cute, the big blue body and the big eyes"), but even she didn't like the name. Another citizen complained that "there must be some venerable symbol of Atlanta culture that bespeaks our heritage as well as our future." Even as a symbol of the future, he said, "I prefer to believe the future holds something a little more inspiring for us than an amorphous blue blob." A recent arrival added, "Just moving here from the North, I was expecting so much more. I was expecting something representative of the South, like southern hospitality, which is known throughout the country, not some animal that no one knows what it is or what it's about." Exactly. (The man who said that, by the way, is black.)

It wouldn't have been hard to come up with something better. I can do it myself. So Georgia, like the rest of the South, is no longer a rural kind of place and you don't want to use the obvious peach, or peanut? OK, I can live with that. Colonel Rebel (the little Yosemite Sam–like figure usually shown saying "Forget, Hell!") is underemployed these days, and so is Chief Nockahoma, who used to pitch his tepee in the Braves' outfield, but even I can see that those guys would have some drawbacks, so let's just stick to animals.

One Atlantan suggested roadkill, but maybe it's not cuddly enough to be commercial. A great choice, a symbol rich in associations, would have been Br'er Rabbit: the trickster figure of African American folk culture, lovingly exploited by a white Atlanta newspaperman and now known worldwide, thanks to Walt Disney. It's almost a metaphor. But if he wouldn't do (and it might be misunderstood), then how about Pogo Possum? I think it was Roy Blount Jr.—if not, it should have been—who suggested once that Pogo was an appropriate mascot for the entire South, and Pogo's even a Georgian, from just down the road in the Okefenokee Swamp. He's cute, he's smart, he's lovable, he's marketable, he's native, and nobody has to ask, "What is it?"

But no, Atlanta has stuck us with this meaningless, embarrassing *nothing*—in Union blue, no less. Every nation gets the capital it deserves, I guess, but what has the South done to deserve Atlanta?

Anyway, pay attention. I bet you'll be hearing more about the struggle for the soul of the 1996 Olympics—more precisely, the struggle about whether they are to have any soul.

III
Fools' Names and Fools' Faces . . .

Parmley's Law (Rated R)

That's right. Parental discretion advised. It's hard to write about twentieth-century culture in terms suitable for innocent ears.

The other evening, some of us were sitting around watching *Blaze*, the movie in which Paul Newman portrays Governor Earl Long of Louisiana. If you haven't seen this good-humored adaptation of stripper Blaze Starr's account of her love affair with the governor, you might want to hotfoot it down to your video rental store and check it out. It has a lot to offer, including some new uses for watermelon.

As we were watching, I was surprised to discover that some of the younger folks in the room assumed the story was fiction. Sic transit gloria Earl. Actually, the movie stays pretty close to the historical facts, although in a few instances it conflates Earl with his brother Huey, and it borrows at least one good line from the stump speeches of Georgia's Gene Talmadge. (The original went, approximately: "You've got three friends in this world, and don't you forget it. You've got the Good Lord. You've got Sears and Roebuck. And you've got Eugene Herman Talmadge from Sugar Creek, Georgia.")

Anyway, the movie's mostly true, even when not accurate, if you take that distinction. My principal reservation is that the star is too good-looking. Earl wasn't a toad, exactly, but he was no Paul Newman. On the other hand, I remember Blaze Starr from my misspent college youth, and she really was a knockout. It turns out she's still practicing her art thirty years later: she even appears briefly in a dressing-room scene in this film.

Earl's downfall wasn't entirely due to his having taken up with a stripper. This was Louisiana, after all, where a majority of white folks recently voted for a tax-evading sex-manual author who has been known to celebrate Hitler's birthday. But, at the margin, Earl's love life probably didn't help his career. We may have here another instance of the law first formulated by my buddy Parmley. Parmley's Law states that nookie corrupts. (Absolute nookie, of course, corrupts absolutely.)

Parmley's Law applies outside the South, too. Ask Gary Hart (although, come to think of it, Miss Rice was an honors graduate of the University of South Carolina). But Southerners may do this kind of thing more flamboyantly, perhaps because we still believe in sin. As well be hanged for a sheep as a lamb, or something like that. Anyway, about the time I'm ready to conclude that they don't make 'em like Earl Long anymore, something amusing happens.

Take Virginia, for instance. The governor, Douglas Wilder, got a lot of good press initially, even being touted as vice-presidential material after only a few weeks in office. Some of our Democrats down here are getting desperate, it seems, and they wanted to portray Wilder as an old-timey Southern Democrat—that is, a patriot and fiscal conservative—who just happens to be black. And perhaps there's something to that. The governor does voice some home truths rather well, as when he observed, "It's more apparent than ever before that our two-party system is becoming a competition between the party inside Washington and that new party, the vast majority of Americans who live outside." It was Wilder, too, who first turned abortion rights into a winning issue by casting it, cleverly, as a government-interference fight. (Harvey Gantt took the same tack when he ran against Jesse Helms, and a North Carolina newspaperman suggested this television ad: "This is Willie Horton. If he raped your daughter and she became pregnant, my opponent wouldn't let her get an abortion.")

But, anyway, within a few months of being elected, Wilder got in trouble for using a state plane to go see his new girlfriend. Since the lady in question is the ex-wife of America's richest man, the governor may have just been hustling for campaign contributions—and there are worse ways to do it. On the other hand, the lady is also (are you ready for this?) a former nude dancer. Some Virginians joked that the Old Dominion did indeed have a "Wilder administration," but those who had been promoting Wilder as a traditional sort hadn't exactly had nostalgic references to Uncle Earl in mind.

Meanwhile, about the same time, in Nashville, it came to light that the mayor, the putatively Honorable Bill Boner, had become engaged to a young lady roughly half his age. The damsel is named Traci Peel, and it would be wonderful if I could report that Miss Peel, ah, does. Alas, she's an aspiring country-music singer, not a stripper, but give her a few points for a first name that ends in "i". (Joe Bob Briggs used to evaluate the Dallas Cowboy cheerleaders by that criterion: the zenith, as I recall, was something like a seven-i year.) And that really is the mayor's name.

Now, I wouldn't be making fun of this happy couple if it weren't for the fact that Mayor Boner was still living with his wife. True, this was wife number three, and third wives, as a rule, ought to have figured out that their husbands are men who are not afraid of commitment. Still, it must be awkward to be married to someone who has given another woman a 2.2-carat engagement ring and who sometimes appears on stage to accompany her on his harmonica. It must be even more awkward when your husband's fiancée tells a reporter that he can—well, that he can "sustain his passion" for seven hours. (Miss Peel is supposed to have said that in the course of a telephone interview, adding, "Not bad for a forty-seven-year-old man"—whereupon a male voice came on the line to say: "Forty-six.") When asked what she thought of her daughter's boyfriend, Miss Peel's mother, Junior (that's right: her father's name is Fred), said: "Why, he's a wild and crazy guy—just like us!"

This being Nashville, the Boner affair gave rise to a number of songs. First off the mark was a WLAC disc jockey, whose "Ballad of Bill Boner" includes such lines as "For seven hours of heaven, will he go straight to hell?" Most Nashvilleans seemed to be having almost as good a time with the story as Bill and Traci, until it was picked up by *People* magazine, *USA Today*, and the TV tabloid *A Current Affair*, at which point respectable Nashvilleans got concerned about their city's image. (So trite, folks. Come on: if you've got it, flaunt it.) One concerned citizen wrote another song called "Bill Boner, Won't You Please Resign?" and even my friend Mona snarled that the former congressman "should have stayed in Washington where he belongs."

What's more, Traci and Bill finally got embarrassed. The mayor said that things had been drawn "out of proportion," and Miss Peel phoned a radio call-in show to denounce the press for making the mayor "look like an idiot" and Nashville "look like *Hee Haw*." "It's a sad, sad day," she said, "when they have to mock our leaders." (Which reminds me of my buddy Eugene's maxim: "When I want a leader I reach for my tackle box.") Traci also accused the media of damaging her career, although she subsequently performed daily at the Tennessee State Fair. At last report, Phil Donahue was trying to get the beleaguered couple to tell their story on his program, but they had split for Hawaii to wait for the mayor's divorce to become

Parmley's Law (Rated R)

final. If nothing else, this shows how things have changed in the last thirty years. When Earl Long needed a rest, they put him in a mental hospital.

In This Corner . . .

As I write, it is mid-July 1990 and the Senate race between Jesse Helms and Harvey Gantt isn't nearly as hot as the weather here in North Carolina, where it was ninety-nine degrees in the shade this afternoon. To judge from the phone calls I've already had from inquiring Yankee reporters, though, Helms-Gantt is shaping up as the big morality play of the fall. Assuming both candidates stay out of jail, our little old state ought to become the focus of right much national attention. That's not surprising, because from a major-metro point of view our election is great melodrama, as good as anything professional wrestling has to offer:

> In this corner, the defending champion, the Darth Vader of American politics, friend of Third World dictators, homophobic foe of artistic freedom, Senator No himself: Jesse Helms of Monroe, North Carolina.
>
> His challenger, from Charlotte, North Carolina, representing the New South and the forces of light: the first black student at Clemson University, the first black mayor of Charlotte, now possibly the first—

Well, who knows? The political handicappers around here don't give Gantt much chance, and neither do I, for reasons I'll get to. But it's early yet, and Gantt has already confounded the oddsmakers by handily defeating his opponent in the Democratic primary runoff, a race that was supposed to be much closer. (Remember when David Dinkins and Doug Wilder did less well than the polls had predicted and we heard all sorts of unflattering speculation about why white people who say they'll vote for a black man, don't? Well, apparently lots who said they wouldn't vote for Gantt, did. Explain *that*, Daniel Schorr.)

Gantt "has done a great deal, probably more than he himself realizes, to establish respectful communication across sensitive barriers in human relations." He "has demonstrated that he knows a thing or two about human nature, and, more important to our way of thinking, that he is sincere." Those observations were offered by— well, by Jesse Helms, commenting for a Raleigh television station in 1963 on Mr. Gantt's application to Clemson University. Helms was comparing Gantt favorably to James Meredith, calling the two men "a study in contrasts." (I guess you could say they still are: Meredith works for Helms now, while Gantt is trying to unseat him.) The relentlessly Democratic *Raleigh News and Observer* turned up that morsel, probably intending to embarrass Helms by quoting him as having said good things about his opponent. The quotations, however, could as easily suggest that Jesse Helms has never been as simple or predictable as his image in some circles suggests.

Anyway, the young Clemson architecture student has grown up to be a politician much in the mold of Virginia's governor Douglas Wilder. Like Wilder, described by my buddy Hal as "the least threatening black man since the Mills Brothers," Gantt is personable and well-spoken. Like Wilder and unlike, oh, say, Jesse Jackson, Gantt has held public office, having been elected mayor of North Carolina's largest city by a biracial coalition. (He was defeated for reelection when the fickle electorate voted in Charlotte's first *female* mayor.)

Gantt also resembles Wilder in that he has kept his distance from the Rainbow Coalition. He said once that "we don't need Jesse Jackson's help," by which he probably didn't mean "we need Jesse Jackson's help like a case of ringworm," but that's true enough. When Jackson's old buddy Louis Farrakhan came to Charlotte to preach whatever the Islamic equivalent of a revival is, he invited Mr. Gantt to attend, but the candidate arranged to be out of town. (He had to be in California for a meeting of the National Organization of Women, which is probably a slight improvement, electorally speaking.)

The conventional wisdom has it that a Democrat can win statewide in North Carolina these days only if he gets 40 percent of the white vote. Terry Sanford got 46 percent, which put him in the Senate. When our governor Jim Hunt ran for the other seat, he got 38 percent, so he had to go earn an honest living, if you can call practicing law earning an honest living. Given those numbers, I think Gantt is a nonstarter.

Not because of his race, though. Sure, NPR will find some white voters to say that they won't vote for Gantt because he's black. But it's a mistake to assume that these folks would vote for a white

Democrat with Gantt's convictions and credentials. Just as any Democrat can count on better than 90 percent of the black vote right now, any Democrat with Gantt's baggage—leave his race aside—is going to have problems with a great many white voters.

There is, to start with, what a Raleigh reporter once called "the Mecklenburg thing." Mecklenburg County—that is, Charlotte—simply isn't very popular with folks in the rest of the state, largely because Charlotteans do little to disguise their conviction that the rest of us are a bunch of yokels. Running for statewide office from there is like being from Atlanta and running in Georgia—no, worse: Atlanta has a lot more voters than Charlotte. Having been mayor of the place may hurt Gantt at least as much as it helps him.

Gantt is also going to have trouble disguising the fact that he is what passes around here for a liberal. So far he hasn't even tried. The other day, for example, he volunteered that he's against capital punishment—thereby disagreeing with a solid majority of the voters, black and white, Republican and Democrat. When even Diane Feinstein has adopted the basketball wisdom that execution is the key to winning, it isn't clear why Harvey Gantt felt obliged to have *any* position on that issue. After all, he won't be able to pardon anybody.

Gantt has assembled a campaign staff with impressive credentials. His pollsters, for example, used to work for Pat Caddell. He has hired a fundraiser and field organizer who used to work for John Glenn and who has served as "Director of Women for the state of Ohio" (whatever that is). His press secretary is a woman who most recently did the same job for Willie Brown, speaker of the California State Assembly. And his "media consultants" are the New York City firm that worked for Jim Hunt when he lost the Big One to Helms in 1984; one of the two "account executives" (that's what they call them) handling Gantt is a woman named Mandy Grunwald, who's supposed to be some kind of hotshot.

Now maybe you're thinking that sounds like a slick, professional operation, and obviously someone in Charlotte thinks so. But it's more likely that you see the problem, which is that this is a carpetbag enterprise. It probably won't work: not because Tar Heels dislike outsiders, but because New York account executives usually don't know diddly-squat about the South. Worse, they don't know that they don't know.

I play poker with a crowd that includes a couple of conservative Democrats—sort of the northern spotted owls of American political life—and one night a while back these guys got to talking about how to beat Jesse Helms. They agreed that you can't win by trying to portray him the way the Yankee press likes to, as evil incarnate. For starters, that concedes that he is an important and powerful figure: the Prince of Darkness may be the kind of stud you want on your side up there in D.C. Besides, too many voters know that that picture isn't accurate. They may not agree with Senator Helms, but they know he's a gentleman, and honest. As George Bush says in some television ads, you always know where Jesse stands (which is more than can be said for "Lips" himself these days). *Esse quam videre*, the state motto says: "To be and not to seem." That's Jesse. He's just a little more outspoken than your brother Butch, who thinks pretty much the way he does. You saying Butch is evil?

In This Corner...

No, the way to beat Helms, my friends agreed, is to make him a figure of fun. Once that happens to someone, he's through. Ask Jerry Ford. Ask Dan Quayle.

Certainly that's true in the South. Consider Jim Folsom: as long as Alabamians were laughing *with* him, they kept him in office; when they started laughing *at* him, his vote percentage dropped to the single digits. The same thing almost happened to Ross Barnett. Somewhere one of Barnett's advisors offers an engagingly candid account of the time Barnett, in mid-campaign, walked into an airplane propeller. Before the candidate reached the hospital, his staff had hastily confected a cover story in which the propeller had mysteriously started up and attacked him. I mean, people already suspected the man was dumb.

When my friends began to "Lester Maddox" Jesse (as they put it), most of what they came up with had to do with his getting the big head up there in Washington and losing touch with his roots. "Textiles going to hell, tobacco going to hell, and he's up yonder having lunch with goddamn Central Americans"—that sort of thing. The nastiest line, probably too rough for a thirty-second concerned-voters-speak television spot but just right for a whispering campaign: "You know, Jesse keeps talking about homosexuals. Now, you know that ain't right. Something *funny* 'bout a man that talks about homosexuals all the time. He's been in Washington too long." (When he heard that, my boogie-woogie piano-playing buddy the Reverend Billy Wirtz instantly dashed off a campaign song, a Glenn Campbell parody called "Genitals on His Mind." I won't quote it in this genteel context, but I have encouraged Billy to apply for Arts Endowment support.)

There is just enough truth in the line my friends were developing that it might sting. The fact is that Jesse does get steamed about some foreign-policy and cultural issues that few folks back home care about much. Those issues may go down with his national constituency, and it's not that many people here disagree with him, they just don't get as worked up as he does. The homosexual conspiracy is a case in point. Like international Communism, it's a rather theoretical concern in these parts. Sure, we turned out two thousand people in Chapel Hill for a statewide Lesbian and Gay Pride March, but, heck, three thousand people turned out the day before for the opening of Interstate 40 to Wilmington.

Anyway, the senator's admirers don't have to worry. My smart-mouth poker buddies aren't running the Gantt campaign. That's being done by Mandy Grunwald and her friends, who will probably go head to head with Helms on no-win issues like capital punishment and Arts Endowment funding. So I conclude, anyway, from what happened when one of my anti-Helms friends, finding himself in Charlotte, presumed on his credentials as a longtime Democratic campaign worker to stop by Gantt headquarters and offer the visiting Yankees some free advice. He outlined the Lester Maddox strategy to a young woman on the candidate's staff. He even sang a few bars of the Reverend Billy's song. But the woman was not amused. "We certainly intend to portray him as weak and ineffectual," she sniffed, "but Jesse Helms is not laughable!"

My friend realized at that moment that he was wasting his time. He says he should have figured that out earlier, when he walked into Gantt headquarters and was invited not to smoke.

Doctoring King

Back in 1990, you may recall, the *Wall Street Journal* reported that Mr. Martin Luther King Jr. became Dr. Martin Luther King Jr. the old-fashioned way: he plagiarized. The editors of the King papers had discovered that King's Boston University dissertation includes lengthy, unattributed excerpts from other people's work. When the *Journal* broke the story, that fact had been known to the editors for three years or so, rumors had been circulating in American academic circles for over a year, and the story had even been mentioned in print in 1989 by the *London Telegraph*, so the question of why it took our watchdog press so long to break it is an interesting one that we might explore some other time. Right now, though, I'd just like to reflect on what King's act of plagiarism means, and what, if anything, should have been done about it.

I hope it's obvious that this was bad news. No patriot should have been happy to hear it, just as none should have been happy to learn about Watergate. As a nation, we're cynical enough already. Soon we won't have any heroes left at all, and a nation needs heroes. It's true that we set ourselves up for this disappointment with our ill-considered haste to put King in the American pantheon, but that doesn't make it any less of a disappointment. Going too far, too fast, with King's canonization had already produced a bunch of wiseguy schoolkids, and I hated to see them confirmed in their juvenile scorn. I hated even more to see the wounding of the innocents who had believed what they were told: that King was not just a great leader of his people, but an admirable man in all respects.

We also saw some pretty sorry disingenuousness and self-deception from a few folks who ought to have known better, as they tried to make excuses for King. Before the plagiarism story broke in the press I was at an academic conference where it was circulating. (One man recalled that Andrew Young once complained that every time he, Young, tried to discuss King's dissertation with him, King was too busy. Now we knew why.) Nothing was said about the story in the conference's public sessions, but it provided a fascinating subtext for some papers and discussion by speakers who knew that we knew what they were talking about. One historian, for instance, spoke of the tradition among black clergymen of "voice-merging"—that is, of borrowing each other's sermons without attribution. He seemed to be suggesting that this is a Black Thing; a rich, vibrant, oral tradition thing; a you-white-folks-wouldn't-understand thing. After the story was made public a few commentators tried this line, going on to draw the implication that plagiarism is a white concept and that objecting to it is evidence of narrow-mindedness, if not of racism.

This slanderous rubbish should be even more offensive to blacks than to whites, and fortunately many people said so. (Right, one columnist wrote of "voice-merging"—and adultery is "wife-merging.")

In any case, cribbing sermons isn't a black thing. It is, if anything, a clerical one. When one fellow I know studied fifty white fundamentalist preachers in North Carolina, for instance, many of them owned up to having borrowed or adapted sermons. In fact, three actually volunteered that they had preached sermons by Martin Luther King. (Or so they thought.) One historian at our conference cited a sermon preached by King that he had adapted from Harry Emerson Fosdick—and that Fosdick had taken without attribution from Phillips Brooks.

The problem, some of us feel, is that there's an important distinction between a doctoral dissertation and a sermon. Sermons are meant to persuade or to edify, not to show off the preacher's originality; if someone else's words are more effective than one's own, why not use those words? But a dissertation is written to show that the writer can make an original contribution; if the candidate doesn't write it, what's the point?

That's how we old-fashioned guys look at it, anyway, but a literary scholar at this same conference tried to set us straight by observing that poststructuralist theory has brought into question the very idea of authorship. I'll try that line if this essay offends anyone:

> I didn't write this, you understand? There's nobody here. You have constructed the author yourself. If you don't like what he says, tough.

Say it won't work? Well, it didn't work for Martin Luther King either, and it was soon abandoned. Even poststructuralists get ticked off when someone fails to cite them, and those of us without advanced literary training just *will* persist in thinking of plagiarism as theft. I don't think King would have denied it, either. As I read the evidence, he had a healthy sense of sin; when he did wrong, he didn't try to pretend it was right. Give him credit for that.

But this revelation let us see that some other people weren't so discerning: the authorities of Boston University, for instance. BU set up a committee—what else?—and after dithering awhile it concluded that there was nothing to be done about this plagiarism. The *New York Times* had long since prejudged the outcome of its deliberations, saying that no action should be taken, since neither King nor his dissertation advisor was alive to defend the case. Maybe there's something to be said for that, but I'm cynical enough to believe that the evidence would have doomed anyone else, dead or alive.

What should the university have done? Well, it's too late now, but here's what *I* would have done.

First of all, the degree should have been revoked. This wouldn't have been punishment for King's folly and dishonesty so much as just a consequence of it—recognition that the degree hadn't been earned, that it had been awarded in error for work that hadn't been done. In other words, this would have been an annulment, not a divorce. But no self-respecting university should allow someone to keep a degree awarded for someone else's work. Why that's so shouldn't have to be explained to professors and it may be impossible to explain to anyone else, but I'll try.

Start with the fact that most academic men and women don't write for money, or fame, or any of the usual rewards, at least not in the usual sense. Many people find that hard to believe, but it's true. As a rule, our primary reward is acknowledgment of our contributions to scholarship, however meager. Footnotes are the closest scholars and researchers come to immortality; ideas and discoveries are what some of us have instead of children. It follows that plagiarism is like kidnapping. It's the unforgivable academic offense.

Of course, some would say that in the larger scheme of things—in the "real world," so called—plagiarism is pretty small potatoes. The *Wall Street Journal* took this man-of-the-world line itself, in a self-congratulatory editorial a couple of days after its newsbreak, and for better or for worse it's probably true. Surely most Americans other than academics do find plagiarism far less reprehensible than adultery, and King's reputation seems to have survived news of the latter more or less intact. If polls of college students can be believed (and there's no reason why they shouldn't), perhaps a majority have plagiarized themselves; no surprise, then, if most folks are inclined to view King's plagiarism as youthful indiscretion, like Ted Kennedy's law school episode.

And, actually, youthful indiscretion is probably exactly what it was. When young Marty King cribbed someone else's work, he didn't know he was going to grow up to be the conscience of the nation and role model to the ages. I presume he planned to be just an ordinary semicorrupt Southern preacher like many others, black and white, before and since. Greatness was thrust upon him when he happened to be in the right place at the right time. But the fact is that he was there, and he had the gifts the situation required, and he changed the world. How many BU graduates can say that?

So in my view BU should have emphasized that its degrees mean something by revoking the one given to King for work he didn't do, but it should have simultaneously awarded him a posthumous honorary doctorate, for what he *did* go on to do. Dr. King would still be Dr. King, but in recognition of his accomplishments, not someone else's. And Boston University would have shown that it knows the difference between right and wrong.

Seeing the Wizard Off

A historical sense can be a wonderful thing. Someone recently reminded me, for instance, that when Christianity was as old as Islam is now, the Inquisition was going full tilt. When Islam gets to be two thousand years old, he suggested, maybe it'll be as guilt-ridden and effete as Christianity has become. I find that comforting, don't you?

In November of 1990 I called on history to console a friend who'd recently moved to Baton Rouge and found himself dismayed by the gubernatorial contest between Edwin Edwards and David Duke. When he wrote that having to choose between a candidate known as "the Silver Zipper" and another billed as "a Nazi for the Nineties" made him uncomfortable, I pointed out that whoever won wouldn't be the worst governor Louisiana ever had; in fact, he probably wouldn't even be the worst governor in living memory. For some reason, that didn't cheer my buddy up.

Boy, was I wrong when I used to complain that Southern politics have become boring—wrong that they're boring, and wrong to complain. I will stay after class and write five hundred times: "Boring is not necessarily bad."

What went awry in the land of dreamy dreams? Just a few years ago, James Moffett, head of the Louisiana Council for Fiscal Reform, was telling the *Wall Street Journal* that "a modern era of politics is fixing to evolve" in his state, yet here was a Baton Rouge Junior Leaguer saying in the *Washington Post* that she was going to vote for Duke because, unlike Edwards, he wouldn't last more than four years in office and maybe somebody would shoot him sooner than that. She wasn't the only Louisianan talking wistfully about the ".38 caliber recall" that took out Huey Long. How did matters get that out of hand?

The problem, of course, went back to the primary, when roughly two-thirds of the voters voted against each of the three major candidates. In each case the majority was right. When Buddy Roemer, the Democrat-turned-Republican incumbent flake, proved to be as inept at campaigning as at governing and came in third, he set up the Edwards-Duke contest.

Now, not even National Public Radio tried to present *that* as a straight-up morality play. In bed with the oil and chemical companies, a gambler and womanizer, oft-indicted (though ne'er convicted), the former governor is an anachronism, a caricature of the sort of pol our nation's newly puritanical press corps eats for lunch. Edwards, whose sense of humor is the best thing about him, told reporters he wasn't going to talk about Duke's past "because he might talk about mine," and there's a lot there to talk about. Many Louisianans had simply never dreamed of voting for Edwards under *any* circumstances, and it apparently took them awhile to realize that voting for the Wiz because you couldn't abide the Cajun Prince would have been like taking a blow-torch to your case of athlete's foot.

In some ways the national attention made it worse. The networks and newsmagazines, like the horrified Louisiana business community, were almost daring Louisianans to vote for David Duke, and that was a mistake. You don't dare Southerners to do anything you don't really want us to do. For every Louisianan who was embarrassed by what the readers of the *New York Times* were thinking, I'm sure another was tempted to vote for Duke just to show he wasn't chicken.

Besides, Duke wasn't exactly wrong on "the issues." Most Louisianans agreed with him on those—at least those issues he talked about. So did lots of folks outside Louisiana (40 percent of Duke's campaign funds came from out of state). For that matter, so did I. And so did many black Southerners, as the polls have been saying for some time, and as the Clarence Thomas hearings could have taught us, had we not been distracted by Anita Hill and the Atlanta Braves. (By the way, *how about those Braves?* They almost avenged the burning of Atlanta, didn't they? There's something I want to say about them, but I'll come back to it.)

As I was saying, lots of black Southerners are every bit as conservative as David Duke was talking, on the issues he was talking about. It isn't just whites who want welfare reform, and crime control, and lower taxes. But it's remarkable that even 4 percent of Louisiana's black voters could bring themselves to pull the lever for a former Grand Wizard, even one who says he now talks to Jesus every day.

A lot of white Louisianans weren't ready to do it either. Newspapers all over the country got a chuckle out of the bumper stickers that said "Vote for the Crook: It's Important," but three out of five voters did just that. True, Duke got 55 percent of the white vote and no doubt we'll be hearing that he lost because of black bloc-voting, but he would have had fewer white votes if blacks hadn't turned out so strongly against him. Either (1) blacks vote their interests or (2) white fear of black power is allayed. Whichever: Duke loses.

Basically, the numbers suggest that Edwards won because he picked up three-quarters of the Roemer voters, most of them conservative white Republicans, I'm sure—people who had to swallow hard to vote for Edwards, but did it, when the chips were down. Partly this was snobbery: country-club Republicans don't want to be governed by a low-life rabble-rouser with a cheap nose job. (True, political life-forms don't come much lower than Edwin Edwards, but at least he's amusing.) Partly, the polls showed, it was also economic concern. Corruption is expensive, but the Edwards campaign argued that a Duke victory would be even more costly, making it harder to recruit everything from factories and tourists to players for the LSU football team. (At the end, Duke was reduced to saying, in effect, "Would *not*.") Surely even more important, though, was the recognition that some things matter more than "issues." Things like, for instance, sin. The American people have always known that, even if political junkies tend to forget it.

Yes, Jesus consorted with sinners, and he may even consort with David Duke. We have to believe that no one is beyond redemption, and maybe there are Baptists willing to take Duke's word that he's found it. Those of us from less forgiving traditions, though, would like more evidence than just some testifying.

Duke talked about his "youthful indiscretions," and obviously he has learned discretion somewhere along the way, but that's not the point. Some "indiscretions" call for more than regret, they call for penance—lots of it. Some of us think a repentant Nazi ought to be off working with lepers or something, not running for governor. It looks as if that view is shared by a good many Louisianans. Enough of them, anyway.

Oh, the Braves? Yeah, look: what is all this stuff about the tomahawk chop? Let the spoilsports from the American Indian Movement take their whining to that sanctuary for guilt-ridden liberals with a football team called the Redskins. Down in Atlanta, even Jimmy Carter was doing the chop. So was Hanoi Jane, although she came up with a more sensitive version, sort of a tomahawk pat. The Reverend Joseph Lowery of the Southern Christian Leadership Conference told ESPN that he could see the Native Americans' point: after all, he said, if the team were the Atlanta Negroes and all the fans waved little switchblades, he'd be annoyed. Well, OK, but he went on to say that folks wouldn't like it if the team were the Atlanta Rednecks and fans waved little nooses.

Uh, Reverend Lowery? Excuse me? You want to rethink that? I mean, that might offend some folks, but it wouldn't offend *rednecks*. I know guys who could really get into that.

The Texas Wild Card

One evening in the winter of 1991, my buddy Eugene and I were shooting the breeze while we sort of half-watched the new, cityfied *Hee Haw*. It's not the sort of show you want to watch alone, and my wife, a nose-breather, won't watch it with me. Eugene had just finished telling the one about the difference between Fidel Castro and a jockstrap (you really don't want to know) when he volunteered that if he lived in Michigan or someplace he might vote for David Duke for president.

I asked him what Michigan had to do with it. (I don't always follow his thought processes.)

He said, "I wouldn't want to make North Carolina look bad."

That made sense, in a way. But Eugene is a patriot who hasn't forgotten World War II, so I asked him why he'd even consider voting for the boy Nazi—even if he lived in a state he wouldn't mind embarrassing.

"Well, I probably wouldn't do it. But who *do* you have to vote for to put a stop to this stuff?"

Of course, I knew what "stuff" he meant. The president we both voted for had raised our taxes, after saying he wouldn't. He signed something that can be distinguished from a quota bill only by the eye of Faith. His Justice Department was trying to reinstate *Plessy v. Ferguson* in Alabama higher education, and using what Eugene calls the "Vote Right Act" (as in, vote right or we'll change the rules) to create Bantustan congressional districts in North Carolina. Thanks to him, our sickly industries face more regulation than Jimmy Carter ever dreamed of, and he even came up with a me-too health-care proposal that threatened to combine National Health efficiency and fee-for-service prices. Even in foreign affairs, where the president was supposed to know what he's doing, he sucked up to the dictator of Communist Russia a lot longer than he had to, and he arranged the demise of a few hundred thousand Iraqis, none of them named Saddam Hussein. He had just put a smarmy junk-bond king on his campaign finance committee, the kind of thing that confirms everyone's worst suspicions about Republicans. That's just for starters, and without even going into what he *hadn't* done.

So, yeah, I knew what Eugene meant. You could say that George Bush was a disappointment.

But give him credit, I said. It looks like we're finally going to get an Elvis postage stamp.

Eugene nodded. "There is that."

Besides, I asked, who else are you going to vote for? Bill Clinton? The guy whose wife dissed Tammy Wynette?

"Naw," said Eugene, "he ain't nothing but Jim Hunt with a sex drive." (I guess you have to know North Carolina's governor, but maybe you can work backwards.)

We were sitting there feeling pretty blue about all this, when some old weepy country song came on the TV to remind us that there are worse things in life than politics gone bad.

How small of all that human hearts endure
That part that kings or laws can cause or cure.

Sam Johnson's words, but a pure country-music sentiment.

Still, I wasn't surprised when I ran into Eugene a few months later and found him sporting a Ross Perot button. What do you know about Perot, I asked him.

"Not a damn thing," he said. "That's the beauty part of it."

Well, that appeal won't last. Soon we should all know a lot more about Mr. Perot. He may decide not to run after all, or he could be becalmed in the single digits where most independent candidates wind up; as I write, though, the polls show this political cipher, basically a "none of the above" candidate, giving Clinton a run for second place nationally, and leading both Clinton and Bush in Texas. This could be even more entertaining than *Hee Haw*.

One thing that's already fun is watching responsible commentators explain that, yes, Perot's candidacy is amusing, but sooner or later we're going to have to get serious. Guys, Eugene *is* serious. When he stops and thinks about it, he's (all together, now) *mad as hell and not going to take it anymore*. When the sixties radicals chanted "Smash the State," Ross Perot wasn't what they had in mind—but, for Eugene, he'll do. Now that the Soviet threat is gone, reckless voting seems less dangerous, and the answer to the question "How much worse could it be?" isn't that clear anymore. So maybe government wouldn't work with Perot as president. You got a problem with that?

Perot's appeal isn't ideological. Who knows what his ideology is? Does he have one? Who cares? In this respect he's like our last serious nonpolitician politician, Dwight Eisenhower. (Russell Kirk, you may remember, defended Ike against the John Birch Society by saying that he wasn't a Communist, he was a golfer.) Perot certainly has *opinions*, on everything from high school football eligibility to abortion, but he presents them and probably sees them as simply "common sense." If enough voters see them that way, too, he could go far.

No, Perot is, if anything, an *anti*-ideological candidate, with an attraction for those who are disgusted not just with government but with latter-day politics, with constant public yammering and wrangling about rights and principles.

Take Eugene again. They say a Middle Eastern moderate is someone whose motto is "Death to Extremists"—well, Eugene could buy that. He's certainly not a liberal and you'd call most of his views conservative, but he's not *a* conservative, and he doesn't like most people who are. He's still a registered Democrat, so he couldn't have voted for Pat Buchanan if he'd wanted to. But he wouldn't have anyway. As far as Eugene is concerned, anyone who is on Sunday TV and isn't a preacher or a pro football player is part of the problem. As he sees it, the fact that both liberals and conservatives deprecate and dislike Perot is a big point in the man's favor.

Something else Perot has in common with Ike is that he's thought to be politically inexperienced. Politicos and political junkies seem to be puzzled and annoyed when voters find that charming. How *dare* he, you can almost hear them saying. Where are his *position papers?* Now, in fact, a billionaire government contractor is no more likely than a General of the Army actually to be *virgo intacta*, but Perot might do well to fake it. A. L. Rowse tells of a candidate for the Oxford University seat in Parliament who won hundreds of votes on the strength of one line in his campaign leaflet: "Agriculture. I know nothing about agriculture." It might work for Perot, too. If nothing else, not knowing how government works means that how it works is probably not your fault.

Then there's the Texas thing. Some sophisticates just *will* see Perot as an untamed gunslinger from flyover country. They prefer their Southwesterners to be Yalies like George Bush or Bill Clinton. It would be embarrassing to watch Perot go after those cosmopolitan votes, just the way it was with Lyndon. If he's smart—and I've never seen it suggested that he isn't—he'll treat his origins the way Hilaire Belloc treated his religion when he ran for Parliament in 1905. "Gentlemen," Belloc told a public meeting, "I am a Catholic. As far as possible, I go to Mass every day. This [taking a rosary from his pocket] is a rosary. As far as possible, I kneel down and tell these beads every day. If you reject me on account of my religion, I shall thank God that He has spared me the indignity of being your representative." (Isn't that more manly than, say, John Kennedy's assurances in 1960 to a group of Baptist ministers that his religion wouldn't affect his conduct in office?)

If I were advising Perot, I'd tell him: Don't pander. Don't apologize. Don't explain. It's not the cowboy way. Just run an in-your-face campaign that says: Here I am, a straight shooter who speaks his mind, a straight thinker who isn't afraid of simple solutions, an obscenely rich man who can't be bought by special interests because they can't afford me. Take it or leave it.

But here I am fantasizing about giving advice to a man who's Eugene's candidate, not mine. Me—well, I'll probably wind up being "responsible" again. I mean, who wants the election decided by the House of Representatives? But obviously even I find something attractive about this candidacy, so let me say one more thing about it. Some folks I've talked to profess to find Perot a little frightening. But what ought to scare them is the alienation and frustration, the wrecking impulse, that he's tapping. All things considered, it seems to me that voting for Ross Perot is a pretty harmless way for that to surface.

Bubba Hubbub

As soon as Bill Clinton locked up the nomination, those of us who write about the South for a living started getting phone calls from reporters asking about the meaning of it all, and when Clinton picked young Al Gore as his vice-presidential candidate, the pace really picked up. The last time this happened was 1976, when Jimmy Carter's nomination provoked a rash of Omigod-what's-going-on-down-there stories in the press. Here we go again.

This time, though, the questions are different. This year they want to know whether Clinton and Gore are "really" Southerners. (Nobody asked that about Jimmy.) I confess that I haven't been able to resist ripping off a *Wall Street Journal* line from the 1988 primaries: Al Gore, the *Journal* observed then, was less a Southern candidate than a Washington political consultant's idea of a Southern candidate.

But that's not fair. It's true that Gore's notoriously wooden oratorical style was at odds with the Southern tradition and that he was (as a friend of mine claims to have seen with his own eyes) the kind of guy who puts on his suit coat to go to a barbecue. But Gore's loosened up some since 1988. What's more, whether I like it or not, he really is a Southerner, of a kind, and Clinton even more so.

Not to put too fine a point on it, both men are Southern yuppies, a tribe as numerous as it is little-known outside the South. The trouble is that very few non-Southerners have a repertoire of stereotypes adequate to deal with this relatively new feature of the South's social landscape. So we get nonsense like calling Clinton and Gore the "Double Bubba" ticket. Aside from the fact that Southerners seldom used *bubba* as a common noun before the national media taught us to, the social type that word identifies is not what Clinton and Gore are.

Bubba is simply the latest incarnation of a well-established Southern white male type, what the press, writing about Carter and his associates in 1976, identified and chronicled as the "good old boy." (Daniel Hundley, writing in 1859, called him the "yeoman," and if you don't believe Hundley was talking about the exact same creature, read a fascinating book called *Southern Folk, Plain and Fancy*. I wrote it.) Since Yankee reporters are seldom attuned to Southern social distinctions, however, "good old boy" in their hands stopped being a perfectly useful label for a particular sort of working-class Southerner and wound up being applied to any male with even a trace of a Southern accent. Now the same thing has happened to "bubba."

Look, I don't have the space even to brief you on Bubba's identifying marks, but take this down: Bubba does not belong to a country club. He listens to country songs about *not* belonging to a country club. On the other hand, Southern country clubs are full of gladhanding, presentable guys pretty much like Bill Clinton—maybe not as smart, driven, liberal, or libidinous, but otherwise much the same. Southern college fraternities even used to have an expression for it: Clinton is a classic "face man."

So, sure, Clinton and Gore are Southerners. But they're housebroken—about as housebroken as Southerners can get these days and still be elected to statewide office. I mean, Clinton actually claims that his favorite book is *One Hundred Years of Solitude*, by Gabriel García Marquez. This may be just a pitch for the Hispanic vote, but I'll bet it's the kind of overreaching you sometimes find among the culturally insecure Southern upper-middle class. (It's far better to say that your favorite book is *Blasting for Bass* and let your questioner try to figure out if you're serious.)

And while it's true that both Clinton and Gore are Baptists, I can't believe that Clinton, anyway, is Jimmy Carter's kind of Baptist—

that is, the real thing. Can you seriously imagine a President Clinton praying for guidance, or asking foreign heads of state about their religious condition, or lecturing federal employees about living in sin? If I'm wrong I apologize, but Clinton strikes me as being Baptist the way, say, John Kennedy was Catholic. (It wouldn't surprise me to learn that Gore is a different story, but I really have no idea.)

Given all this, it's pretty lame when Jay Leno makes jokes about "trying to get that all-important *Hee Haw* vote." Those of us who enjoy ethnic jokes at other groups' expense really can't complain (although we can point out that it's roughly like saying Jesse Jackson had to be placated lest the all-important watermelon vote be lost). Still, that crack has the remarkable property of annoying both Southerners who like *Hee Haw* and Southerners who don't. And when Republicans engage in similar badinage, they win no friends for their party or their candidates. Dan Schnur, chief spokesman for Governor Wilson of California, might as well have been on the Clinton-Gore payroll when he said that "Bill Clinton and Al Gore fit in about as well in California as the Beverly Hillbillies. They're like Granny and Ellie May sitting on the back of the truck." When that kind of stuff gets reported back in Carolina it makes even me want to vote for them.

So why *did* the Democrats nominate two Southerners? Well, I guess they couldn't help nominating Clinton after he won all those primaries, but why did they go along with putting another Southerner on the ticket? I think Susan Estrich gave a pretty good answer at the convention when she revised Henry Clay for the 1990s: she's tired of being right, she said; she wants to win instead.

Think about it. Since 1945 the Democrats have won with candidates from Texas, Georgia, and the border state of Missouri (whether Kennedy actually won depends on your view of those Illinois returns), and they've lost with candidates from Illinois (twice), Minnesota (twice), South Dakota, and Massachusetts. See a pattern? Even flatworms can learn with reinforcement like that. (Jimmy Carter's 1980 reelection loss just shows that geography isn't everything.) What's more, a new book called *The Vital South*, by political scientists Merle and Earl Black, argues persuasively that it's almost impossible to win a presidential election these days if you don't at least split the South and strongly implies that enough folks elsewhere share "Southern" views that you can probably win if you carry it.

If you buy that, Gore becomes an obvious choice for the vice-presidential nomination. An all-Southern ticket won't automatically carry the South, but it's a good start. In the first place, Gore doesn't *hurt* Clinton in Dixie, as most of the available non-Southerners would have. In addition, once you get past the fact that Clinton and Gore are both from the South, they're quite different. From a Southern point of view, Gore levels out the potholes in Clinton's résumé very well. Say Clinton dodged the draft? Gore's a vet. Clinton waffled on war with Iraq? Gore didn't. Clinton's too cozy with the Yankees and "special interests" who run the Democratic Party these days? Gore ran against Dukakis and Jesse Jackson in the 1988 primaries. Clinton's wife is a lawyer who puts down Tammy Wynette? Gore's is a blonde homemaker who gets fierce only when her cubs are threatened by degenerate rappers and heavy metal scum. It's not exactly that Gore is the Good Twin, the Anti-Clinton; he's more like the responsible older brother to young Billy, the scamp.

It's just a bonus that Gore also firms up Clinton's ties to several traditional Democratic groups, concentrated largely outside the South. Does organized labor prefer even Jerry Brown to Clinton? Gore's a strong labor man, like his daddy before him. Does Clinton's lust to keep jobs in Arkansas give him a suspect environmental record? Gore's unreadable book reassures the Greens. Say the Permanent Government sees Clinton as a small-state governor with no D.C. experience? Gore *grew up* in Washington. Clinton didn't inhale? Gore did.

Sure, some old-timey Northern Democrats are nervous and resentful about the new Southern Ascendancy. My buddy Doug was at the convention and overheard a couple of delegates discussing in an elevator how uneasy it made them to have to vote for two Southern Baptists; when he asked what if their party had nominated two Jews and he'd said that he was nervous about *that*, a chilly silence descended. It was fun, too, to watch Mario Cuomo try to keep from sneering each of the many times he said "Arkansas" in his convention speech. But what are these bigots going to do, vote for Bush-Quayle? Come on. Most of the pros, at least, seem to agree with Susan Estrich. They'll try to keep their regional prejudices under wraps and hope they get some appointments.

Anyway, it will be interesting to see how the Democrats' Southern strategy plays out. Clinton and Gore are demonstrably the kind of

Democrats who can win elections in the South because, after all, they've won some. It's hard to imagine a Democratic ticket that would run better in the South, unless maybe Gore and Clinton switched places. Is that good enough?

Well, let's do the numbers. First, despite a considerable degree of social and cultural conservatism, Southern blacks are still reliably and overwhelmingly Democratic. With or without Jesse Jackson's enthusiasm, Clinton and Gore will do as well there as any white candidates could. They'll also collect the votes of the small if noisy contingent of moderate-to-liberal white Southern Democrats (many of them migrants from other parts). On the other hand, most Southern wealth is too new to be apologetic, so upper-middle-class Southern whites are almost reflexively Republican these days. These voters will stick with Bush, even though many think he's too liberal. The few remaining diehard Dixiecrats won't vote Democratic either.

As the Black brothers point out in their book, that leaves the choice up to the large body of conservative Democrats and independent voters, many of them white working-class folk (Bubba and his wife, if you insist). These folks voted for Bush in 1988, but tend to be seriously put out with him these days. Many flirted with Perot, and some of them may be ready to return to the party of their ancestors if it makes even the slightest pretense of returning to them. By running Clinton and Gore, it's making that pretense.

Now, it's a safe bet that Bill Clinton won't get most of their votes. But he doesn't have to: a strong minority will do. In early August, a South Carolina poll showed Clinton trailing Bush by a double-digit margin among whites—this at a time when Clinton led nationally by more than thirty points and was even ahead of Bush in Orange County, California. But that same poll showed Clinton with a comfortable lead in South Carolina overall, thanks to the lopsided support of black voters.

The Democrats' problem lately has been that they haven't come anywhere even near the 30 percent or 40 percent of the white vote that they need to win. It's hard to say whether this ticket can turn that around, but Merle Black told me in August about a Democratic party worker who was handing out bumper stickers at a rally in South Carolina. "This year," the man said, "they're going to put those things on the *outside* of their cars."

IV

Tossin' and Turnin', Churnin' and Discernin'

Official State Business

Perhaps you heard the howls (actually, more like hollers) a while back when some hapless Texas bureaucrat proposed that the Lone Star State be known henceforth on its license plates as "The Friendship State." You've got a friend in Pennsylvania, according to that state's plates, but it sounds as if Texans want to check you out first. Texas is, after all, the state where a major-party gubernatorial candidate recently observed that we need to keep our guns because "we may have to march on the government one day if it doesn't straighten out." It's where anti-litter signs say "Don't Mess with Texas." Some of us—not just Texans—believe it's bad enough that the state makes you register your car without making it a medium for tourist advertising.

Actually, though, as Dallas columnist Molly Ivins pointed out, "The Friendly State" probably wouldn't have raised any hackles. Texans *are* friendly, for the most part, and don't mind people's saying so. But many who would have found the adjective unexceptionable somehow felt that the noun was a little, well, wimpy. Last I heard, the sobriquet had been shelved, but the controversy was good for some laughs while it lasted. Ms. Ivins evoked a few of them with reflections on the whole business of license-plate slogans. She suggested, for example, "Oklahoma—Land of Recruitment Violations." Like me, she believes that the only plate a real man would put on his car voluntarily is New Hampshire's "Live Free or Die."

North Carolina's sure isn't one. Our plates say "First in Flight," which some of us believe is too easily construed as "First to Flee." This isn't a happy rendering at best, and it's especially unfortunate given that "Tar Heel" is said to have originated as a reference to the staying power of North Carolina's Confederate troops. Our plates used to say "First in Freedom," which was widely understood to be a reference to the so-called Mecklenburg Declaration of Independence of 1775. It doesn't behoove an employee of the State of North Carolina to comment on the historicity of that event (also commemorated on the state flag), but what we've done is displace a reference to a doubtful but inspiring event to commemorate the undoubted but boring fact that two bicycle mechanics from Ohio made use of one of our empty beaches to test their flying machine. At least "First in Freedom" used to annoy some of the right people, one of whom put masking tape over the slogan—and wound up in court for it, which actually sort of proved his point. "First in Flight" isn't worth covering up.

Anyway, a while back one of our legislators proposed an equally baffling exercise in banality when he introduced a bill to make something called the plotthound our Official State Dog. He was not deterred by our past experience with Official State totems, which has not been altogether happy. Our O.S. Bird, for instance, is the mockingbird, a standing—or flying—contradiction of the state motto, *Esse quam videre*, "To be and not to seem," a bird whose sweet song disguises a foul disposition and obnoxious habits.[1] Our O. S. Flower, the lovely dogwood blossom, comes from a tree that seems to be headed for endangered species status, thanks to a fungus that has killed whole hillsides' worth. (A correspondent for the *Southern Partisan* got a different account from a storekeeper near Asheville: "It's Daylight Savings Time," Mr. Bud Wingo explained. "The dogwoods did just fine until they started taking away an hour of sunlight every year.")

In any case, the plotthound bill didn't get very far, largely because no one had ever heard of this animal. When it was revealed that the creature is German, one commentator asked whether anyone knew what part of Germany it comes from, hinting darkly that we might be about to elevate a Communist dog to Official State status. (This was before the Berlin Wall came down, and most folks around here were still taking a wait and see attitude toward glasnost.) Once the subject was broached, champions of other dogs came forward (the bluetick hound had a number of partisans), and the debate kept our legislature from doing anything foolish for days on end.

For my part, I think we've just scratched the surface here, and I hope our legislators will put their minds to this matter. An O.S. Food, of course: pork barbecue (with tomato optional, to prevent civil war).

1.When this was originally published I heard from a good many Tar Heels, pointing out that North Carolina's state bird is the cardinal. One correspondent remarked that my error was about what you might expect from someone born in New York. In any case, my middle-aged memory failed me—it is my beloved home state of Tennessee that has seen fit to canonize the mockingbird—and as an act of penance I have let the snafu stand.

But that's too easy; we need something to keep our legislators busy for a *long* time. How about an Official State Disgrace? I suggest the North Carolina State University basketball program.

Once you get started, it's hard to stop. Why not an Official State Roadkill? The sleeping drunk is a possibility (North Carolina leads the nation in lying-in-the-road deaths), but if the legislature balks at that there's really only one other candidate. The skunk has a way of pressing its claim, but for sheer numbers the possum has no competition. Other states may feel that they have an equal or greater right to the possum (Texas has the armadillo, of course), but come on: we thought of it first.

And every state needs an Official State Bug. We can leave the boll weevil to Mississippi, the fire ant to Georgia; let the Land of a Thousand Lakes have the mosquito, Maine the black fly, New York the cockroach. North Carolina still has all sorts of possibilities. Some homeowners, for instance, might nominate the termite. Perhaps it would be some consolation when your floor caves in to know that the Official State Bug has been on the job. There's also a case to be made for the black widow spider: most years we lead the nation in spider-bite deaths. (I know, spiders aren't insects. That's why I said "bug.") But my own nominee would be the common tick. We have a special claim to that critter, too, since we're always #1 in Rocky Mountain spotted fever cases. And just think: if we made the tick our Official State Bug, next time we redesign our license plates they could say "First in Rocky Mountain Spotted Fever."

A Mess of Greens

When my secesh batteries need recharging, as they do every once in a while, I go hang out with someone like my Alabama friends Ward and Peggy. When I visited them in April of 1990, we went on a pilgrimage to the First White House of the Confederacy in Montgomery. As we floated down the Interstate in their splendid old Lincoln (which they call a "Davis," of course), Ward told me about a recent Right to Life march. Several thousand Alabamians had arrayed themselves around the statehouse where Jefferson Davis took the oath of office and sung—the Battle Hymn of the Republic. Oh, well.

On the evening of Earth Day a group of us gathered at Ward and Peggy's to recycle some pig. My wife and I had spent the day driving around eastern Alabama and parts of west Georgia, and I'd seen no indication in Columbus or Opelika that anyone was especially lathered about the fate of the planet. Certainly there was nothing to compare to the Yankee and California celebrations depicted at tedious length on cable television. Eufaula and Tuskegee, West Point and Auburn—all had seemed about equally unconcerned on that sunny spring day, and the lack of enthusiasm extended to our supper table. When I mentioned Earth Day, there were some groans, a joke or two, and then a change of subject. I began to wonder: why this Southern disdain for the modern American version of environmentalism?

Yeah, sure, there are New Age, pantheistic, love-your-Mother environmentalists in the South, but they tend to be found in Yankeefied enclaves, or as isolated village cranks. A rock band called the B-52s, for instance, collect money for Greenpeace and for animal-rights groups at their shows. But they come from the college town of Athens, Georgia, and anyway they recently moved to upstate New York, where I'm sure their vegetarianism will be easier to sustain than in a great barbecue town like Athens.

It's not that traditional Southerners don't care about the natural environment. Take a look sometime at the almost lyrical portrait of man as predator presented by a magazine called *Southern Outdoors*. Ward introduced me to that marvelous repository of traditional wood-craft and nature lore, noting that the magazine's ads tend to be for expensive, high-tech, productivity-increasing gadgets like electronic fish-finders, an ironic juxtaposition he especially savors.

Anyway, a number of public-opinion polls show that there really is right much pro-conservation sentiment in the South, and so does the success of a country song called "Pass It on Down," by the group Alabama. But what's out there is just that: sentiment, a sort of anticipatory nostalgia not anchored to much inclination to do anything. When it comes to practice, we Southerners lag behind. At best we seem to echo, feebly and suspiciously, slogans that originated somewhere else.

That's sad, because if you're looking for antecedents for today's environmentalism, for its suspicion of technology, its antirationalism, antispeciesism, and all the rest, you could do worse than to look at some Southerners. As Ed Yoder suggested some years ago in an essay called "The Greening of the South," the old-fashioned "Twelve Southerners" who wrote a book called *I'll Take My Stand* had some strangely modern things to say on the subject.

Now, I should say that no less an authority than Andrew Lytle, the last surviving contributor to that volume, disowns the connection. In a 1983 interview Lytle accused today's ecological activists of sentimentalism and statism, and denied that he and his friends were guilty of either. But I think his memory was playing tricks on him. Certainly some of the Agrarians were less anti-statist than others. Frank Owsley's essay "Pillars of Agrarianism," in particular, advocated legislation that one critic called "kremlinesque." And while no one has ever called Lytle a sensitive New Age guy (a "snag," as some of us call them), I think the young man may have been more sentimental than the old one let on.

Lytle denied, for example, that the Agrarians would have given a damn for the snail-darter. But they weren't polled in 1930, and some of them had at least the premises for getting excited about obliterating part of God's Creation. Consider a passage from the book's introduction. Under industrialism, John Crowe Ransom wrote, "We receive the illusion of having power over nature, and lose the sense of nature as something mysterious and contingent." Or how about this, from Ransom's own essay: "Industrialism is a program under which men, using the latest scientific paraphernalia, sacrifice comfort, leisure, and the enjoyment of life to win Pyrrhic victories from nature at points of no strategic significance." And listen to Lytle himself, calling for "a proper respect and a proper regard for the soil"—not a mere metonym. Lytle even sounded like some of today's more apocalyptic environmentalists when he predicted "a moral and spiritual suicide, foretelling an actual physical destruction."

It would be wrong to extract these views from their religious underpinnings, from the more general piety, more or less orthodox, in which they were embedded—or, more accurately, with which they were entangled. (If anything, true religion seemed sometimes to depend on proper environmental views.) Here's Ransom again: "There is possible no . . . sublimity of religion, which is not informed by the humble sense of man's precarious position in the universe." Or again: "Religion is our submission to the general intention of a nature that is fairly inscrutable; it is the sense of our role as creatures within it." Take that seriously, and the implications put you in some strange company today.

Fifty years later, Lytle said that he and his colleagues believed that nature "was mysterious and to be respected, and we took time to examine it in the world and in ourselves. . . . We knew that land is built up only slowly, and it can waste away in no time at all if not properly tended." Lytle also observed in 1983 that "our attitude toward nature was part and parcel of the kind of life we wanted to preserve. You would naturally not destroy the things by which you made your living."

Now, this may have been true enough for the Agrarians themselves. But they sometimes implied that they were articulating the Southern tradition, and any implication that Southern farmers have been something like instinctive ecologists—well, it reminds me of what a friend calls the "Cronon Indians," a mythical tribe of happy precapitalists who inhabit the pages of William Cronon's book *Changes in the Land*. Call what the Agrarians wrote a trope, if you want to save it, but as an empirical description of Southern agriculture it is, alas, nonsense. Southern agriculture in 1930 wasn't just slash and burn, it was rape and pillage.

Of course, you can explain this by economic necessity. The South's system of cotton tenancy reinforced the biblical injunction to take no thought for the morrow; at least in that respect the applied agrarians of the South were good Christians. But there's more to it than that. Ransom's characterization of industrialism as "the latest form of pioneering and the worst" brings to mind another Southerner who wrote about the pioneering mentality, but who saw it as especially characteristic of rural Southerners. In *The Mind of the South*, W. J. Cash described white Southerners' frontier-style individualism, nurtured by the frontier, the plantation, and Reconstruction. Cash drew compelling pictures of the planter "wholly content with his autonomy and jealously guardful that nothing should encroach upon it," of the poorer whites "as fiercely careful of their prerogatives of ownership, as jealous of their sway over their puny domains, as the grandest lord," and of the whole crowd displaying "intense distrust of, and, indeed, downright aversion to, any actual exercise of authority beyond the barest minimum essential to the existence of the social organism."

In the South, the great impediment to effective environmentalism or even conservation has not been indifference to open spaces, the wonders of nature, and the works of God, but this frontier ethic, which says what a man does with what is his is no concern of yours, and certainly not the government's. Southerners suspect that Lord Melbourne was right when he observed that people who say something must be done generally contemplate doing something damned stupid—and these days it's usually something that expands the power of the state at the expense of individuals and their families.

A Mess of Greens

Two generations after Cash, another Southern journalist described the same attitude, as it has persisted to the present day. Southerners, Roy Reed wrote in the *New York Times*, still "carry in their hearts or genes or livers or lights an ancient, God-credited belief that a man has a right to do as he pleases. . . . A right to go to hell or climb to the stars or sit still and do nothing, just as he damn well pleases, without restraint from anybody else and most assuredly without interference from any government anywhere." As Hank Williams Jr. puts it, "A country boy can survive." Charlie Daniels adds: "If you don't like the way I'm living, just leave this long-haired country boy alone."

Now, ordinarily I admire this attitude, even share it to a degree. As Roy Blount said once, I wouldn't want to live in a place where there aren't bullet holes in the road signs. But Roy Reed spelled out the distressing implications: "It is no accident that the most determined hold-outs against land-use legislation in the United States are country people from the South. They will take care of their own land, and let the next man take care of his. If the next man puts in a rendering plant or a junkyard, that is his business."

Does it come down to a choice between a society where free spirits blight the landscape and poison each other, or one where the state tells sullen but healthy serfs what they must do? I hope not, and it's good to see libertarians and other anti-statists turning their attention to this problem at last. Lord knows I have no answer, but if there is one I suspect that private organizations like the Nature Conservancy and Ducks Unlimited will play an important part.

Let me tell a story that illustrates the kind of cultural jujitsu that can sometimes get you somewhere. I had a friend who used to live about forty miles north of here. Each deer season his seventy acres became a free-fire zone. Scores of hunters roamed his land (as they'd always done before he owned it), firing high-powered rifles at just about anything that moved. Fearing for the lives of his dogs and family, he posted "No Hunting/No Trespassing" signs time and again, only to see the hunters riddle them.

Then inspiration struck. He posted signs that said "Osmond Hunt Club. Members Only." A spooky calm settled on his place, broken only by the sound of his doorbell as a steady stream of very polite hunters stopped by and asked to join. He says he put them all on the waiting list.

Man's Best Friend and Other Brutes

Highbrows who read books like this one may not know a television program called *America's Funniest Home Videos*, but it's just exactly what it sounds like. I bring it up because a story in *Newsweek* a while back reported that the program's staff was surprised to discover regional differences in the tapes that viewers send in. According to a man who screens submissions, the Midwest's FHVs are usually episodes from family life and California's tend to involve "far-out stunts," but Southerners, he said, produce endless footage of "bizarre guys sitting around drinking beer while trying to produce a video." This man singled out one Southern tape for special mention: it showed "a small, stick-wielding child fruitlessly pursuing a frog around a yard as an off-camera voice kept shouting, 'Git it! Git it!' "

I hate to say it, but that sounds about right.

Southerners do seem more likely than other Americans to believe that frogs and other critters have been put here to amuse or otherwise to serve us. I guess I'm a case in point. A reader once wrote to charge me with a pattern of insensitivity to animal rights, and I'm guilty. I have often written with indifference and even with approval about blood sports, the eating of red meat, and other activities detrimental to the welfare of individual beasts. Moreover, I have made fun of animal-rights zealots—partly because they're zealots, but there's more to it than that. I'm afraid I'm being typical.

"Egg-suckin' dog," Johnny Cash sings, "I'm gonna stomp your head in the ground." In what other region does casual violence against animals figure in popular music? No doubt you've seen the bumper

stickers that say "I [heart] NEW YORK," or "CHAPEL HILL," or
"[picture of a golden retriever]." Maybe you've also seen the ones
that say "I [spade] MY CAT." But only in the South have I seen
"I [club] BABY SEALS." There are parts of the country where it
wouldn't be safe to make that joke.

The entry on "pets" in *The Encyclopedia of Southern Culture*
states it simply as a fact that Southerners are "less likely [than other
Americans] to express concern about the right or wrong treatment of
animals or to strongly oppose exploitation or cruelty toward animals."
That entry was written by Margaret Young, a sociologist who studies
interaction between humans and animals. Dr. Young teaches in a
veterinary school, and she's also a professional dog trainer. She does
a good deal of outside work these days as an expert witness in court
cases where people have lost hands or children to killer dogs. She
says that Southerners are less likely to get in this sort of trouble,
because we're less likely to forget that dogs are dogs and don't think
like us. That is, we're less likely to confuse them with human beings.

You could say we have more respect for their doghood; we believe
that dogs should and will do doggy things, that they have their own
part to play in this world, and maybe the next—a part different
from ours, complementary, and, yes, subordinate. Dr. Young says
Southerners are "more likely to express concern for the practical
and material value of animals or their habitat"—that is, for their
use to us.

I'm not a hunter (although I've hunted), but some of my friends
and relations are mighty huntsmen, especially of doves and deer,
which I'm happy to help them eat. It's important to them to eat what
they kill, because—this is significant—it's a form of respect for the
animal. These fellows don't get theological about it, but some of
them could. The most prophetic Southern voice of our time, that of
Wendell Berry, has had some fine things to say about the biblical
theme of stewardship, which licenses the use of God's property, but
insists that we care for it, too. If you don't understand the hunter's
ethic, and don't have someone around to explain it to you, take a
look at a book called *Southern Hunting in Black and White*, by Stuart
Marks, an anthropologist and hunter who spent years in Scotland
County, North Carolina, studying hunters of deer, duck, coon, quail,
and so forth. Each group turns out to be almost a separate tribe, with

its own folkways and initiation rites, and it's weird and wonderful to see them treated by someone whose previous book was about African lion-hunters.

But, getting back to my friends, if you tell one of these guys that a deer has rights, he'll laugh at you. Ask him how he'd feel if he were a deer and he'll explain patiently that he's not. Tell him that he and the deer are one and he might get angry. But suggest that habitat preservation or a lower bag limit this year means better hunting next year, and he'll listen intently. There is a mutual dependence here, although it's not based on identity, or even equality.

The same is true for domestic animals. Margaret Young observes that Southerners are more likely than other Americans to expect household animals to work, to earn their keep. They are subordinate, but their work complements ours and contributes to the common wealth. Horse and rider, hunter and dog, mule and farmer: these symbiotic pairings are rooted deep in the collective memory.

Obviously, Southerners can *like* animals. Old Blue is a legendary good old dog. Old Shep even got himself sung about by Elvis. Another singer has made a song of his daddy's request to his mama to "wake me up early, be good to my dogs, and teach my children to pray." But we value animals as individuals, not generically, and we value them for what they do for us. Dr. Young believes, for instance, that Southerners are relatively more likely to judge dogs on their performance rather than their breeding. Johnny Cash doesn't seem to care about the pedigree of his egg-sucking hound, and in "The Bear" Faulkner celebrates the bravery of a little mixed-breed dog, a "fice." ("Fice" is the origin of "feisty," by the way, and you might want to check out the etymology before you use that adjective as a compliment.)

A life of loyal service can elicit genuine affection. Dr. Young writes that, "while expressing indifference or incredulity toward the idea of 'loving' animals, many southerners form strong affectional attachments to individual animals." These attachments, though based on usefulness, can outlive it. ("Once unable to work, [working dogs] still retain a special status within the household.") But even the best good old dog may not get in the house. ("The key elements of companion animal status are frequently fulfilled without inside residence for the animal.") We may address our dogs as fondly as our children, in other words, but we don't say the same things to them. They're *animals*, after all, and Southern pets know their place.

Look, Southerners have always drawn sharp lines between categories. All traditional cultures do. Black and white, male and female, saved and unsaved, Southerner and Yankee, "quality" and trash, human and beast—we've insisted on these distinctions, God-given or otherwise. We've even gloried in them. We've tempered our boundary-drawing with a pervasive particularism that recognizes considerable variation within categories, but we haven't been comfortable with ambiguity.

Obviously we've overdone it sometimes. Learning to live with fuzzy and ambiguous distinctions is what cultural modernization is all about. That's probably inevitable, in many respects even desirable, and it's certainly well underway in the South. But Richard Weaver was voicing an ancient Southern suspicion when he wrote in "Life without Prejudice" that hostility to society's distinctions often masks hostility to society itself, that confusion of roles and loss of differentiation is exactly the meaning of societal collapse. We need to take those warnings to heart, and to insist on necessary distinctions when they are in fact necessary.

If my description of the place of pets in the Southern household sounds like *Driving Miss Daisy*, it's no accident. Just as racial paternalism is gone with the wind, so in time Southerners may come to believe that animals don't exist primarily in relation to us. Hell, our evolving cosmic consciousness may lead us to understand the essential one-ness of Being (and to talk like New Age Californians). We may come to view "Old Shep" as this century's "Old Black Joe." But that time isn't yet. And if that analogy offends you, you must agree.

Devil with a Blue Dress On

Just down the road from us is Durham, North Carolina, a funky old New South town whose chief contributions to American life probably lie in the areas of piedmont blues music and the mass production of cigarettes. Like any Southern town that has been around for a while, Durham has its odd features. A writer for the *Charlotte Observer* reported a while back, for instance, that four of the seven Americans known to have swallowed their toothbrushes were from the Bull City.

Even odder than that, in some ways, is the fact that this wholesome blue-collar town is home to Duke University. Yet there it lies, its mock-Gothic campus nestled incongruously among the abandoned cigarette factories and the Carolina pines, an institution once best known for basketball, the rice diet, psychic research, and turning down the papers of its most distinguished alumnus, Richard M. Nixon. A physician named H. L. Newbold once speculated in the British journal *Medical Hypotheses* that tobacco baron James Duke founded the place because of neurological damage and depression resulting from pernicious anemia—and that certainly does explain a lot.

Now if someone could just explain the peculiar behavior of some of Duke's literature professors, whose high jinks have been getting so much bad press lately from Dinesh D'Souza and his friends. I often find myself defending the place these days. After all, my wife, her brothers, my godson, and several of my cousins are Duke graduates, my uncle taught there for many years, and several of my friends still do. So I always try to point out that Duke is not only a trendinista stronghold but also something of a bastion of the counterrevolution, the home of some fine reactionary scholars and publications, and the only campus in the country with its own chapter of the National Association of Scholars. It is not beyond salvation.

That said, however, the weird stories just keep coming. In its latest spasm of political correctness (a phrase I was trying to avoid, but can't seem to) Duke has done away with its chapel's boychoir. It apparently did so at the behest of one of the campus ministers, a woman who had never even attended any of the services at which the choir performed but who complained that the group was one of the "subtle and not so subtle vestiges of male privilege" that she has a vocation to extirpate. It's refreshing to see a modern-day cleric promoting orthodoxy of *any* sort, but some of us could suggest more obvious places to start a heresy hunt.

Look, I yield to no one in my concern for women's rights. I care a whole lot more about my daughters' opportunities than about the prerogatives of the couple of billion earthlings who happen to be male, most of whom I don't even know. But this is just silly.

Some splendid music has been written for women's voices, and no one would complain if Duke nurtured a girls' choir of distinction equal to that of its now-late boychoir. But it's simply a fact that the unchanged voices of boys *sound* different from those of girls, or of a mixed-sex choir, and many masterworks of church music were composed for precisely that sound. Moreover, the Duke chapel may well be the only space between Washington and Atlanta truly suited for the performance of such music: it is the nearest thing this world offers to a Methodist cathedral, from the Duke family's heroic tombs to sculpted images by the doorway that include those of John Wesley, Savonarola, and Robert E. Lee.

Choral evensong is one of the glories of the English university tradition that Duke apes in a great many less attractive ways. But a boychoir by definition is not "inclusive," so (we're told) it has to go. If nothing else, this bizarre decision reveals the hollowness of the "diversity" scam, which celebrates the alleged contributions of almost every imaginable culture, no matter how squalid or insignificant, except the historic European one that gave us, among other things, Duke University. No, the dean of the chapel says, "Within the context of Duke University and its goals, values, and mission," having a choir open only to boys is "unfair."

Bull pucky. Last I heard, the Duke basketball team was still all-male. You Dukies want to get *serious?*

An Academic Remnant

As a rule I don't inflict academic shoptalk on my friends. Most aren't college professors, and few things are more tedious than another profession's gossip. Besides, there's no regional angle to this stuff, except that the trendy foolishness currently plaguing American campuses may afflict Southern schools marginally less than those elsewhere (Duke University aside). Still, if you don't know about an organization called the National Association of Scholars, you should. A while back I went to a meeting of that group in New York, and I'd like to tell you about it.

The NAS aspires to be an umbrella group for faculty members concerned or at least annoyed by what's going on around them.

This gives it, to say the least, a broad agenda. At one time or another the organization and its quarterly, *Academic Questions*, have deplored entropy in the curriculum; the metastasis of race, ethnic, and gender studies; the denigration of excellence and Western civilization in the name of "diversity" and "multiculturalism"; the deformation of humanistic learning by tendentious or self-indulgent "theoretical" work; the proliferation of race- and sex-based hiring and admissions policies; and no doubt other enormities that I don't recall at the moment.

Of course, not every NAS member is exercised about all of these issues. Some of us are soft on multiculturalism, for instance. Others doubt the efficacy of imposing a core curriculum on unwilling students, or fear what a core curriculum designed by today's professors might look like. A few try to look on the bright side of literary theory and victim studies. Some (mostly tenured) aren't wild about the alternatives to affirmative action. Others just question whether it's politic for the NAS to bundle all of these issues: after all, the broader the agenda the narrower the constituency.

Still, the issues do tend to come as a package, and from pretty much the same promoters. And most of the NAS program ought to appeal not just to us reactionaries but to liberals of the old-fashioned sort. That's certainly true when the organization steps forward to defend the traditional academic freedoms of speech and inquiry.

It's hard to talk about the threats to these freedoms without sounding hysterical, but they are threatened. That's not new, of course; they usually are. What's new is that the threat these days comes from what we might as well call the left, and that the usual defenders of academic freedom (notably the American Association of University Professors) are strangely supine in the face of what they would ordinarily call McCarthyism.

In my own discipline, for instance, the American Sociological Association was called upon a few years ago to censure James Coleman of the University of Chicago for producing a study of busing with conclusions that were ideologically offensive. At Harvard, when historian Stephan Thernstrom was denounced for "insensitivity" in the classroom, his accusers at first declined to specify the charges further; eventually they produced a list of offenses that included Thernstrom's observing that nineteenth-century Chinese immigrants practiced an "Oriental" religion and remarking that family instability contributes to present-day black poverty.

Now, Coleman and Thernstrom are big boys, bull elephants of the academic jungle, and they weathered these episodes without permanent damage—although they've both become active members of the NAS. But what about students and junior faculty? When the sensitivity police come for men and women without named chairs and international reputations to protect them, a new double standard is applied without shame. Recently a student editor published some stupid slurs on Duke's black cafeteria workers; he was drummed out of office without one solitary bleat from the usual First Amendment fundamentalists. When an art student's offensive painting of Chicago's former mayor in ladies' underwear was torn down—well, actually I think it should have been torn down, but then I feel the same about Mr. Serrano's *Piss Christ*. (Even if Jesus Christ's reputation is on firmer ground than Harold Washington's, how about some concern for the feelings of Christians?) But where were the defenders of the supposed rights of that student "artist"? Hell, he wasn't even receiving NEA funds.

It's probably the ninety-eight-pound weaklings of academia who need the NAS most, and one of the great pleasures of the New York meeting was hearing from some of the Charles Atlases of our profession. One session dealt with the question "Can the Professoriate Reform Itself?" The consensus seemed to be that, no, it couldn't. (One speaker claimed that nothing short of air strikes could reform the Yale Divinity School—a remark given a certain piquancy by the presence of the secretary of defense, who had come with his wife, the chairman of the National Endowment for the Humanities.) Despite this pessimism, though, everyone seemed pretty cheerful. When you hear sense being spoken by people like Coleman and Thernstrom, by Gertrude Himmelfarb and Dean Donald Kagan of Yale—well, you realize that you're not just right, you're in good company.

It's like the famous Asch experiments, which Intro Psych students of a generation ago may recall. Asch asked groups of people to say which of several lines was the longest. The actual subject of the experiment was the last to be asked, after several pseudo-subjects had confidently and consistently made the wrong choice, and often the poor schnook simply caved in and went along with the group. Some just felt it wasn't worth arguing about, but others were actually led to doubt the evidence of their own eyes. A few, unusually suggestible, even saw one of the shorter lines as longest, when the others said it was. Even subjects who made the right choice usually did it hesitantly and apologetically.

Apparently it takes a real hero, or a real jerk—anyway, someone unusually stubborn or arrogant or courageous—to insist that everyone else is simply wrong, even when they obviously are. That's the bad news. The good news, though, is that the presence of even one fellow dissident almost always produced nonconformity. Which is why the NAS meeting was such a heady experience: it was downright exhilarating to be in a room with a few hundred others who also know which line is longest.

It's hard to overstate the political lopsidedness of American college faculties these days. I think it was Thomas Sowell who said that the ideological spectrum usually ranges from left to far left. Those of us with views outside that range are likely to spend our working lives subjected to relentless academic groupthink, usually not so much conscious harassment as just the constant weight of assumption.

Incidentally, the bad guys in this business are not, for the most part, the former student radicals of the 1960s. Those of us who still bear grudges from those days may like to think they are, but we need to be reminded that the sixties are now as long past as the thirties were then. It's sobering to realize that our students see the days of the Free Speech Movement as either a mythical era when giants walked the earth or an irrelevant past that tiresome old fogeys get nostalgic about—either way, an epoch now lost in the mists of time. Sure, some of our old adversaries have now completed their Long March through the institutions and emerged as aspiring thought-controllers. They're doing their best to insure that, a generation from now, scholars who don't share their opinions will be found only in disciplines like poultry science or in colleges named for living evangelists. They're a problem: in particular, they put others' commitment to a depoliticized academy to the test, because it's hard not to want to purge people who would gladly purge you. But, outside a few departments here and there, they're not the *big* problem.

That comes from a much more numerous and influential party of well-intentioned souls who practice what one speaker at the meeting called, after Veblen, "conspicuous benevolence," supporting programs and policies that demonstrate goodwill and correct thought, almost without regard for any other consequences. To those of us who can see which line is longest, for example, it's perfectly obvious that quota systems undermine the self-confidence of their supposed beneficiaries and breed cynicism and resentment in others. That argument needs to be made (probably in an accent other than mine), but it will not move someone who is determined to show that he cares, that he is not "mean-spirited." One speaker at the meeting confessed that this kind of amorphous benevolence almost made him nostalgic for the old-timey academic Marxists, most of whom at least had some sense of intellectual rigor and believed there are more important questions than whether people feel good about themselves.

Anyway, maybe—just maybe—the tide is turning. Let me tell a story.

Ten or twelve years ago, my department chairman got a question-naire from something called the Gay and Lesbian Task Force of the American Sociological Association asking (1) how many members of our department were openly gay or lesbian and active in gay and lesbian causes, (2) how many were gay or lesbian, but not politically active, and (3) how many he thought *might* be gay or lesbian. (My colleague, a brilliant statistician and demographer, is a Brahmin from Kerala who takes a rather detached view of American academic politics. He photocopied the questionnaire and sent it around, essentially asking us to volunteer.)

The NAS meeting reminded me of that episode. Deviants of the sort the NAS speaks for are also a vastly outnumbered and sometimes persecuted minority, although I wouldn't want to push the analogy too far. (Nobody's suggested quotas for us yet—and I hope nobody does, because I'd be tempted.) We, too, come in varying degrees of outspokenness. Not many are willing, at least not yet, to be active in an organization like the NAS. But there are more who make little secret of sharing our views. They may not feel as strongly about them, or they may feel they have better things to do than fight for lost causes (I often feel that way myself), but their mere existence makes an important contribution, as the Asch experiment suggests. It may be wishful thinking, but I believe there are more such witnesses than there were a decade ago. Ironically, the politicization of our campuses may have brought this about. People who constantly ask "Which side are you on?" are sometimes going to get an answer they don't want.

Perhaps even more encouraging are what I take to be signs that a growing number of our colleagues think straight in private. They really know which line is longest, in other words, but aren't yet ready to be disagreeable about it. Those of us who *are* ready have all had colleagues sidle up to us, glance furtively about, and whisper that we're right about something. My favorite example is the friend who told me in 1984 that he was going to vote Republican—but asked me not to tell his wife. I've even had a few colleagues tell me that they read my column in the magazine *Chronicles*. You can bet they get their subscriptions at home, not at the office, but it's a start. One of these days they may be ready to come out of the closet.

Trivializing Rape

Recently I picked up our student newspaper to read this sentence in a front-page story: "Statistics show that one out of every four UNC females will be sexually assaulted while in college." Wow. The University of North Carolina has roughly 15,000 undergraduates (leave the graduate students out of it), something over half of them female. So that would mean, oh, 450 or 500 assaults on previously unassaulted undergraduates every academic year, or about 16 or 17 a week. Surely I'd have heard about this. I mean, if it's that bad, anyone who sends a daughter to Chapel Hill is making a big mistake. Forget UNC: put her in purdah. At least give her a sidearm—she'll have more use for Smith and Wesson than for Strunk and White.

I suspected that what we had here was a factoid. I figured there'd be a long, long trail a-winding from the *Daily Tar Heel* to anything that could be considered a reliable source, but I resolved to follow it. For you, dear reader—for you.

In the event, the trail could have been longer. The student reporter told me that she got the figure from a friend, who got it from a book assigned in a women's studies class. (Strictly speaking, she said, it applied to American colleges in general, not UNC in particular, but several sources had told her that UNC was not unusual in this respect.)

Well, OK, but I still didn't believe it, so I went to the library and got the book *Feminist Fatale: Voices from the "Twentysomething" Generation Explore the Future of the Women's Movement*, by Paula Kamen. It sent me to another book: *I Never Called It Rape: The Ms. Report on Recognizing, Fighting, and Surviving Date and Acquaintance Rape*, by Robin Warshaw. That cited several articles reporting a survey of 6,100 undergraduates at 32 colleges, conducted in 1985 by Mary P. Koss, Ph.D., with support from the Center for Antisocial and Violent Behavior of the National Institute of Mental Health. Back to the library one last time, for an article by Dr. Koss and two coauthors, all from Kent State University, called "The Scope of Rape," published in the *Journal of Consulting and Clinical Psychology* in 1987, where I finally found something resembling data.

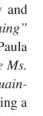

Trivializing Rape

The point of all this bibliographical trivia, by the way, is just to show how these things work. A student reporter cites a fellow student who cites a pop feminist tract which cites a journalistic report which finally cites some serious research. To get the obvious questions answered (How was the sample drawn? What was the refusal rate? What were the differences between different kinds of schools? How were rape and attempted rape defined?—just for starters) you have to dig.

I'll tell you what I found in a minute. First, though, some observations.

Once upon a time, back in what my teenager calls the "Dork Ages," we knew what rape was, and it was serious. As a matter of fact, until the Supreme Court interfered with us, first-degree rape was a capital offense in every Southern state. That may have had something to do with the relative absence in my youth of what has come to be called "date rape."

I believe it really was rare. Some time ago the columnist Hal Crowther wrote that he not only never heard the term when he and I were in college, he never heard of the phenomenon. This wasn't entirely because of our male friends' respect for women (although there was more of that around than you'd suppose, to read most feminist accounts of the period); it also had to do with self-respect. Real men didn't force themselves on women.

Hal's recollections squared with my own, although I wondered if he and I just knew unusually well-behaved guys, or if the rapists of our acquaintance simply weren't talking. But then I read an essay by Florence King on the subject. "Date or acquaintance rape is a phenomenon of the sexual revolution," she wrote, "and so foreign to my experience that I can't think of anything to say about it. In my day, when a woman told a man to stop, he stopped." Thank you, Miss King, for that testimonial to our generation.

So what's happened since 1965 or so? Well, aside from scrapping the death penalty, we've changed the definition of sexual assault. By law, in most states, it now includes not just sex acts accompanied by physical force or threats of violence, but also those made possible by the victim's diminished capacity due to drugs or alcohol. I'm glad that's illegal—don't get me wrong. But maybe we ought to call it something else.

Let me tell a story. A while back, at a hearing in these parts about discrimination against homosexuals, the manager of a gay bar (call him "Jim") told a remarkable tale. He said that he met another man in a convenience store; they picked each other up (or however these things work) and repaired to a nearby motel where, ah, nature took its course. Then, to Jim's surprise, his new friend attacked him with a pair of scissors, calling him names that reflected unfavorably on their shared sexual orientation. When Jim escaped and went to the police to report this assault, the policeman he told about it reminded him that sodomy is illegal in North Carolina and suggested that he might want to think twice about pursuing the matter. Believe it or not, the point of Jim's story was that both the policeman's attitude and the epithets his assailant used were evidence of ubiquitous "homophobia," requiring new civil rights laws to protect its victims.

Spare me. Come on, is it really hard-hearted to deny this guy 100% USDA Choice victim status? Is it unreasonable to observe that someone who gets naked with strangers in rented rooms is taking his or her chances? I'm awfully glad it's not my political party that has to pretend to take this kind of thing seriously.

Anyway, consider the question "Has anyone ever tried to take advantage of you when you were drunk?" If every woman who answers it "yes" is now to be counted a victim of sexual assault, inevitably we're going to devalue the term. Sure, whatever grubby sexual transaction takes place between a couple of commode-hugging drunks is wrong, and if it's not "consensual" it ought to be criminal, and you can call it rape if you want to. But I'm sorry, it's not something I'm going to lose a lot of sleep over. Victimhood, like the dollar, isn't what it used to be.

Now, please, I'm not suggesting that drunk or drugged women "deserve it." Being drugged is prima facie evidence of illegal activity and so is being drunk for anyone under twenty-one, but even criminals have rights, and just being stupid isn't a crime at all. We old-fashioned guys believe there's no excuse for what, yes, we still call taking advantage of a woman, and we don't object to punishing a man who does it. We also believe, however, that there's a qualitative difference between that and raping her at knifepoint, and if the law doesn't recognize that difference it really *is* an ass.

But Suzanne Fields, writing in *Heterodoxy*, a combative new chronicle of campus folly, observes that when a *New York Post* editorial called for a legal distinction between stranger rape and sex preceded by "consensual activities" like drinking, visiting a man's hotel room, or walking with a stranger on a deserted beach at 3:00 A.M., it caught hell. I can believe that. As I write, our local D.A. is being harassed by the thought patrol for a memo to our police pointing out that North Carolina law requires some evidence of resistance for a rape charge to stick. As the law stands, just saying "I don't think we should be doing this" isn't enough. In fact our D.A. wants to see the law changed to add the crime of third-degree rape, but that doesn't satisfy those who want to blur distinctions and conflate all involuntary sexual activity (and possibly, as Suzanne Fields suggests, to portray rape as the paradigm for all heterosexual relations, but that's another story).

It's clear where we're headed. Increasingly the rape theorists are invoking the nebulous and slippery concept of "psychological coercion." According to *Heterodoxy*, a pamphlet at Swarthmore already defines "acquaintance rape" as "ranging from crimes legally defined as rape to verbal harassment and inappropriate innuendo," and Stanford's Judicial Affairs Office interprets coercion, outlawed by the student code, to include "belittlement" or "verbal pressure." Just as sexual harassment (a real and serious problem that, incidentally, did exist in my youth) has been trivialized by being stretched to include all sorts of unpleasant behavior and bad manners—and, in some versions, to be defined in the mind of the "victim" (if you feel harassed, you are harassed)—so we seem to be on the way to defining as a rapist some clown whose idea of foreplay is a couple of hours of begging. Fortunately, I'm not the first to observe that this really does demean women, who aren't all *that* helpless.

But what about that statistic (I hear you say)? Well, to make a long story short, I never did find the "one in four while in college" number—surely you'd have to ask graduates to get that, or do some tricky extrapolation from undergraduates' reports—but what I did find makes it plausible, given the study's definitions. Fifteen percent of the undergraduate women surveyed reported sexual encounters since age fourteen that met the study's definition of rape, and another 12 percent reported encounters that met its definition of attempted rape; 17 percent had had one or the other sort of encounter in the past year. There really is a lot of nastiness out there, and something has indeed gone very wrong since my college days. But not all the nastiness is what most of us think of as "rape." Not even most of its victims think of it that way. According to Suzanne Fields (who must have seen some data I missed), 73 percent of the women the study said had been raped didn't think they had been—plainly candidates for reeducation—and 42 percent had intercourse with the "assailant" on a later occasion.

By the way, although the study's definition of sexual assault sticks to encounters that most states would treat that way, it did ask about sex acts resulting from "continual arguments and pressure," a wooing strategy rephrased at one place in the text as "coercion," at another as "menacing verbal pressure." You get the drift.

It's a shame that the study muddies the water this way, because the situation it documents is bad enough. By the FBI's more stringent definition, which requires force or threat and doesn't include the alcohol and drug scenarios, 8 percent of these young women had been sexually assaulted in the past year. If the same ratio holds, 11–12 percent will be assaulted at some point while in college— not "one out of four," but more than enough to be alarmed about. And there's no reason to question the sample. It's true that students at religious colleges were less than half as likely to have been assaulted, and religious colleges were underrepresented in the sample, but not enough to make a major difference in the estimates.

It's interesting that the study also included a similar sample of college men. Five percent of them acknowledged behaviors in the previous year that the FBI would consider rape or attempted rape: 1.8 percent and 3.3 percent, respectively. The difference between that 5 percent and the 8 percent of women who reported having been assaulted is no doubt partly due to underreporting (even most rapists are smart enough not to trust a researcher's promise of anonymity), but it may also reflect the fact that many of our campuses have become stalking grounds for predators from "the community." Campus security is a genuine problem, and one that might be easier to address than acquaintance rape—but it doesn't carry quite the same satisfying ideological freight.

Anyway, to return to my diatribe about blurring distinctions, the real problem, I think, is that treating all this stuff as equivalent makes it less likely that we'll come down hard on the genuine badasses. Even the folks who get most het up about date rape don't seem ready to *do* much about it. A couple of years ago, for instance, Donna Shalala, the politically correct president of the University of Wisconsin, was asked by *Time* magazine what her school was doing about the problem. After some conventional blather about preventing it by education, communication, and counseling, President Shalala said this: "If it occurs, you've got to be as tough as possible. In some cases throw someone out of school, force him into some kind of education program." Right. At my own school, in 1989, rape was made a violation of the Student Code. Big deal.

President Shalala's idea of how to get tough with rapists illustrates the sort of wooly-mindedness and sentimentality that we encounter all the time on modern college campuses. Why, after all, should a university have a policy about rape? We don't have one about homicide. If we're really dealing with rape, not just second thoughts the next morning, we're talking about crime. "Throw someone out of school"? Naw, let him stay in school—if he can figure out how to do it while pulling, say, ten to twenty years of hard time. And *there's* an "education program" for you. From what I hear about our prisons, chances are the swine will acquire a better understanding of rape from the victim's point of view than he ever imagined was possible.

Incidentally, just a couple of months after the *Tar Heel* reported that a quarter of our female students will be assaulted, a letter-writer to the weekly *Spectator* upped the ante. "In a college town such as Chapel Hill," he wrote, "one-third of the women will face a rape or sexual assault situation during their residency." If that rate of increase keeps up, we'll hit 100 percent in a little over a year and a half.

Locally Owned and Operated

How about three news items from a typical week in a Southern university town, just to get the old motor warmed up?

Dateline Chapel Hill, May 1990:

—A new law against urinating on the sidewalk resulted in a dozen arrests, nearly all of them of beer-drinking students too pressed to wait or too drunk to care. Formerly such revelers were charged with "littering"—but the Age of Euphemism is over.

—The school board lowered the required grade average for admission to the high school Honor Society, to provide "a level playing field" for all students. One board member observed that "black students might not have an equal chance at society membership because of peer pressure to do poorly in school." (Excuse me: I thought the whole point of an honor society was to honor students who do well—not just better than you'd expect.)

—A new yuppie muffin shop opened—a chain operation. Unless I grossly underestimate the local muffin hunger, it should drive the old, locally owned yuppie muffin shop out of business. That's what happened with the premium ice cream shops and the frozen yogurt places. And a locally owned bookshop was recently kicked out of the mall to make space for B. Dalton, which (we were told) would make the mall more easily valued when the owner wants to sell. Thus, man, born free, is found everywhere in chains. (Sorry.)

About that last item: it turns out that the mall's present owner is the pension fund of KLM Royal Dutch Airlines—which gives me a

theme for a tirade. Some of my colleagues at *Chronicles* magazine
are given to ranting about foreign ownership of U.S. enterprises; let's
take that logic one step farther.

First of all, though, let me make it clear that I'm not knocking
outside investment in underdeveloped economies. I grew up in what
amounted to a branch-factory company town in East Tennessee, and
our Eastman Kodak plant was certainly good for local pocketbooks.
If it didn't contribute a hell of a lot to the community other than some
noxious fumes and several thousand jobs—well, the people who had
those jobs contributed greatly, and without Eastman there wouldn't
have been much of a community in the first place.

*Locally
Owned and
Operated*

But Eastman built that factory and created those jobs. That's a
different proposition from what has been going on lately in North
Carolina, where outside corporations have been grabbing up existing
enterprises, more often than not destroying jobs, or at least moving them somewhere else, in the process. Recently Morgan Stanley looted Burlington Industries so shamelessly that even the *Wall
Street Journal* was shocked. Once-proud Liggett and Myers is now
owned by a British outfit that runs it almost as an afterthought—
and ghost factories in downtown Durham are the result. After RJR
merged with Nabisco, the insufferable CEO of the new enterprise
moved its headquarters from bucolic Winston-Salem to the fleshpots
of Atlanta, allegedly because his wife found us Tar Heels insuffi-
ciently urbane. And homely old Piedmont Airlines, also formerly of
Winston-Salem, got itself bought by USAir; now its headquarters are
in Pittsburgh, its flight attendants all sound as if they grew up in
Cleveland, and its in-flight magazine no longer carries inspirational
articles by Methodist bishops.

I'm agnostic on the economic aspects of these deals (although
I can't believe they're good for North Carolina). But the cultural
and civic consequences are surely dismal. Private philanthropists and
middle-sized corporations with local ties tend to spend their money
near to home, and often in admirable ways. One day, for instance,
I suddenly realized just how many of the things I still like about
New York were provided or maintained by the Rockefeller family's
money: the Cloisters, the Palisades, the Museum of Modern Art,
Washington Irving's house on the Hudson . . . the list goes on. Just
so, no citizen of North Carolina can be indifferent to the benefactions

of the state's great textile and tobacco families. When their money got old enough, these folks showed as much noblesse oblige as anyone could ask. Besides, they lived in the state and had an interest in North Carolina's welfare and its reputation. But does anyone suppose that the managements of Morgan Stanley or RJR Nabisco give a damn about North Carolina's churches and hospitals and universities and public libraries and art galleries? How can we rely on private philanthropy—and restrict the Arts Endowment to commissioning equestrian statues of dead generals—when all the philanthropists have left town?

The problem with these megaconglomerates is that they tend to replace the community-oriented philanthropy of provincial corporations and private capitalists with centrally determined do-good policies that address whatever the fashionable cause du jour may be. For example, I've got a copy here of something called "Making a Difference," a "Social Responsibility Report" from Time Warner, the corporate result of the merger of Time, Inc. and Warner Communications. The pamphlet seems to define social responsibility as a matter of trendy environmental concern and sensitivity to the fashionable pressure groups. Prominently listed among the company's contributions to the common weal are putting "safe sex" leaflets in albums by Warner Brothers artists Madonna, Lou Reed, and the B-52s, and allowing Madonna to appear at "Don't Bungle the Jungle," a rain forest benefit concert.

Now, I've got a more than incidental interest in what Time Warner is up to, because a few years back Time, Inc. bought Southern Progress Corporation, publishers of *Southern Living*, the fabulously successful house-and-garden magazine. Some of us never did like the idea that the largest-circulation Southern periodical now reports to New York, and this pamphlet makes me even more suspicious. "The broad agenda for Time Warner's community investments is set at corporate headquarters," it begins, and of course that's so: you can't let individual field commanders declare their own wars. But *Southern Living*'s special relationship to its hometown of Birmingham—which has helped to make that city one of the few that get more pleasant each time I visit—now survives only by permission of Time Warner headquarters.

So far I don't think the change of ownership has been reflected in the magazine's content, but I fear the worst. I haven't felt this way since I learned that a New York company owns Rebel Yell whiskey. Yankee buy-outs of our tobacco and textile companies are one thing, but our identity is a different matter. Excuse me for sounding like a French Minister of Culture, but it's scary to think that my friends at *Southern Living* now work for the same bosses as Madonna, Neil Young, k.d. lang, and Snoop Doggy Dogg.

I hope I'm wrong, but keep an eye on *Southern Living*. If all this means is a few public-service ads for environmental causes—well, there's nothing wrong with that. But if it means propaganda for safe sex, watch out. Southerners know there's no such thing. Any country music fan can tell you that.

Taking the Tenth

It's not easy, being a decentralist.

A while back, a concerned citizen asked Carl Fox, our district attorney, to listen to 2 Live Crew's nasty album "As Nasty as They Wanna Be." Professor Henry Louis Gates Jr., then of the Duke English department, had just argued in the *New York Times* that the album's lyrics were a valid expression of the vibrant folk culture of African Americans, but our D.A. wasn't buying it. He's black himself, but he didn't have the advantage of a Duke education, having gone instead to the state university (where, as a matter of fact, he took a course from me). Carl thought the record was both misogynistic and obscene, as it most certainly is, and announced that he would prosecute any record dealer who sold it in his jurisdiction.

Guess what? His phone started ringing off the hook, and before very long he backed down. He said that most of the voters who elected him appear to believe, "shockingly so, that the only thing that should be restricted is child sex."

I'm glad he's shocked, but he's probably right about voter opinion. I'm afraid putting up with obscene rap songs is one of the prices we have to pay for the dwindling pleasure of living in Chapel Hill. Those of us who believe in local control have to take the bitter with the sweet. Communities really ought to decide these matters for themselves, even if they decide wrong.

But our legal system doesn't make that easy. The Supreme Court now includes "contemporary community standards" as part of the definition of obscenity, but my experience as an expert witness in a pornography trial—expert, I hasten to add, in social research methods, not pornography—leads me to conclude that the Supremes have screwed up again. (They mean well—but, then, they usually do.)

Let me tell you about that trial. The Charlotte police busted two out-of-staters who owned and ran an "adult" video-rental shop, and their lawyer, a big gun from Detroit, commissioned a bunch of surveys to show that their merchandise didn't violate Mecklenburg County's standards. I was hired to vet the methods used, and the surveys did show, essentially, that most Charlotteans believe their neighbors ought to be able to watch any damn video they want, even one rented from a Yankee-owned smut shop. In other words, Charlotte seems to have no standards, at least in this matter.

You might think that would settle it, but think again. The prosecutor argued that the jury, as representatives of the community, could ascertain the community's standards by introspection, and when the judge ruled the survey evidence inadmissable on technical grounds, they had to. The jury was heavily weighted (literally) with middle-aged black women who looked like good churchgoers to me; how the defense lawyer ever let *that* happen I can't imagine, but it didn't surprise me when they concluded that a couple of the films in question were obscene. (They found that several others, indistinguishable to the untutored eye, were not, and I still can't decide whether that was Solomonic or just nonsensical.) Last I heard, the decision had been upheld on appeal and the defendants were looking at something like seven years in the pokey.

I actually feel sorry for them, but not because I have any problem with Charlotte's trying to close their business down. In fact, if I lived in Charlotte, I'd be for it, in a casual sort of way. I don't think "Debbie Does Dallas" is what Thomas Jefferson had in mind—although with Jefferson you never know, do you? I don't have any problem with harsh sentences for "victimless" crimes, either, although it's true that lots of murderers these days don't pull as much time as these guys are going to.

But there *is* something wrong when it takes an elaborate and expensive trial to figure out, not what you've done, but whether it breaks the law. Consulting "contemporary community standards" is a great idea, in principle, but even if you get them right (by survey research, say) they can change. And if jurymen are going to tell you what the standards are by examining their consciences, they're going to change from jury to jury. It seems to me that laws ought to be written so you can know when you're breaking them. Most other countries have obscenity laws like that, but lately our courts won't let us have them. It has become so hard to figure out what you can forbid and what you can't that the temptation is just to give up and allow *anything*.

Here's where decentralization could come to the rescue, if we'd let it. If the federal courts want to tie themselves in knots about what can be sent through the U.S. mails, that's OK. But if Charlotte's elected government wants to forbid over-the-counter traffic in video nasties, what's that to the rest of us? If dirty old Charlotteans can drive to Chapel Hill and buy anything short of child pornography, or mail-order it from an 800 number, or get it from the inevitable black market, what is it even to them? It seems to me that the citizens of Charlotte should be able to use their representative institutions to establish "contemporary community standards" of decency in their common, public life—especially if they can do pretty much what they please behind closed doors. Anyone who really wants to live where he can buy *Animal Lovers* at every convenience store can move. What's wrong with that?

True, we have a meddlesome federal government that recognizes no limits on its authority and is prepared to make all our states and communities look alike in various ways. The Tenth Amendment was almost a dead letter even before the states' pigging out at the federal fisc gave the federales the lever they needed to dictate everything from drinking ages and school-bus colors to speed limits and cable-television rates. But they haven't seen fit to impose uniformity in every respect—even in some fairly important respects—and maybe we could use those chinks to make a case for allowing diversity in other areas.

It seems to be settled, for example, that it's no business of mine, as a North Carolinian, if Louisiana lets grocery stores sell liquor, or Massachusetts runs a lottery, or Nevada permits brothels. It also appears that Californians can legalize sodomy and (for the time being) that Georgians can forbid it, without interference from the rest of us. That's all fine with me. How about you?

Well, if you're still with me, how about if Utah rethinks polygamy (again), or Oregon wants to legalize marijuana? What's your beef?

I can argue this case with some sincerity because—to get right down to it here—I do just barely care what other states do. As far as I'm concerned, Californians can outlaw North Carolina's cigarettes, we'll outlaw their pornography, and everyone will be healthier. Californians who want their smokes and Carolinians who want their smut can move, smuggle, or do without. That's what the Founding Fathers had in mind, or should have.

Of course you have to draw the line somewhere—at slavery, for example. We settled that. Some individual rights do trump corporate liberties. Even a North Carolinian wouldn't get to be indifferent to, let's say, a neo-Aztec revival of human sacrifice in New Mexico. And those who see abortion as human sacrifice without even a propitiatory motive, like those who see its absence as a form of slavery, won't find the Hatch Amendment a satisfactory resolution of that troublesome question.

No, decentralization wouldn't mean tranquility in every respect. In fact, it's a recipe for *more* conflict of a wholesome sort: conflict about where to draw the line. I seem to recall that William Buckley wrote once that much of libertarianism is foolishness, but that our politics would be healthier if we were actually debating whether to sell the lighthouses. Just so, I think we'd be better off if the debate about states' and communities' rights were taking place well to windward of where we are now.

Alas, though, it's not just liberals who want to centralize power in D.C. My principal complaint about the so-called neoconservatives is their enthusiasm for federal solutions to problems. Sure, they're real problems, but so is the metastasis of federal intrusion, especially since half the time it wouldn't work right anyway. Chester Finn, late of the U.S. Department of Education, has said a lot of smart things about education, for example, but he said a monumentally dumb one when he called recently for a national curriculum. Principles aside, he needs to reflect that such an innovation could as well be used for experiments in multicultural empowerment as for the sort of little civics lessons he has in mind—and in fact the first seems more likely to me than the latter.

Neocons may be especially unreliable on this score, but they're not alone. Some time back, for instance, my state's senior senator was calling for a federal law to punish HIV-infected health-care workers who knowingly treat patients. Now, that might make a pretty good *state* law. We could pass it in North Carolina, our HIV-positive doctors and dentists could move to states that hadn't passed it, and—well, we'd see, wouldn't we? But I can't begin to imagine why Senator Helms thought that was an appropriate subject for federal regulation. There must be something in the water in Washington.

That would also explain why, when Representative Henry Hyde of Illinois got annoyed at attempts by the sensitivity police to ban "hate speech" on some of our more fashionable campuses, he jettisoned his limited-government principles and introduced a bill that would have forbidden private colleges and universities to interfere with student speech. That idea stinks to begin with. Conservatives should have better things to do than protecting students' rights to call each other "nigger" and "faggot." Sometimes colleges and universities *ought* to regulate what their undergraduates say. *My* ideal college would throw students out if they didn't behave like ladies and gentlemen, and calling each other hateful names would do it. Of course, so would occupying the dean's office or disrupting Republican politicians' speeches—even Henry Hyde's.

But the important, apparently forgotten point is that these are private, voluntary institutions we're talking about. What they do in this respect—even when they do stupid, wrongheaded things—should be no business of the government's. Religious schools should be allowed to forbid blasphemy, if they want to, and if Duke wants to become the Bob Jones of the left, it's entitled. It's a free country, as we used to say (back when we also said "sound as a dollar").

But we decentralists can take comfort from the fact that, however futile and unavailing our views may seem to be, time is really on our side. I attribute my sunny and equable temperament to that. Come what may from Washington, I'm calm. Grants for performance artists, pay raises for Congressmen, minority set-asides, New World Orders—none of this discourages or depresses me because, whatever detestable enormities our would-be leaders visit upon us, I comfort myself by reflecting on this simple truth: Anything that tends to bring the federal government into disrepute isn't all bad.

V
Under Southern Eyes

What I Did on My Vacation

August of 1990 found our family on a blue highway tour of the Northeast, angling across some of the remoter parts of central Pennsylvania and upstate New York to Lake Champlain, crossing on the ferry for a few days in Vermont with my expatriate sister. From there, one day, we nipped up to Montreal to extend fraternal greetings to the Quebec secessionists.

Just kidding. They had their hands full with Mohawk irredentists at the time. But whatever the outcome of Canada's latest constitutional crisis, I do wish the Quebecois well. Their culture's worth saving, and they're absolutely right to be concerned about the threat to it from the surrounding Anglophone world. To be sure, Quebec's stringent French-only sign laws make it look as if you're in a French-speaking country, but I was disappointed, on this first visit, at how easy it is to get along in English.

Even the signs seem to compromise when it really matters. For instance, on the superhighway, perhaps wisely, signs explain in both French and English that some westbound lanes become eastbound for the afternoon rush hour. Similarly, a hand-lettered sign on a public toilet said both "Pas fonctionale, eh?" and "Out of order, dude."

But not everyone replied in English to my halting French, and a fine lunch of sausages and pommes frites at a businessmen's bistro in Vieux Montreal led me to wonder once again why the French from Saigon to New Orleans are so good at table. It's still far more interesting to cross the border in Vermont than in Michigan, and although it's really none of my business, I'd like to see it stay that way.

Most French-Canadians would, too, of course, so they're now demanding protections that other Canadians may not be willing to give them. As an Anglo reporter for the Canadian Broadcasting Corporation complained to me, "They want to be treated as if they make up half the country." Well, a Southerner ought to recognize the doctrine of the concurrent majority when he encounters it, and this Southerner, at least, sympathizes.

If push comes to shove, will Quebec take a walk? Plainly some separatists have been looking for an excuse, and it may be that Canada is finally as untenable an idea as, say, the Soviet Union.

Not long ago *Time* magazine was saying confidently that prosperity had undermined Quebec nationalism, but au contraire, mes amis, it may merely have given the secessionists the resources they need to pursue their goal effectively. Montreal is now an impressive city, Quebec is an impressive province, and far sorrier excuses for nations are voting in the UN. Americans should be grateful for the fact that Canada has been a good neighbor for a long time, but surely it's not for us to say what's best for another democracy. If Canada did dissolve into its constituent parts, would it be bad for anyone other than the bureaucrats in Ottawa? I wonder.

Coming back through Vermont from Montreal we stopped in St. Albans to read the historical marker commemorating the October day in 1864 that twenty-two Confederate troopers appeared in that town to give some startled New Englanders a taste of what was going on in Georgia at the time, robbing three banks and stealing some horses before fleeing to Canada. (You take your victories where you find them, OK?) I'm sorry to say that in 1990 nobody in St. Albans gave our North Carolina license plates a second look.

Speaking of license plates, on that same drive I realized that I hadn't noticed any vanity plates in Vermont. I was working up a theory about thrifty Yankees who don't see the point of spending good money to tell strangers what wild and crazy guys they are, when I was passed at high speed by two cars in a row. The first said "SNAKE," the second "OUTLAW." I felt right at home. (Shortly after that I saw a pretty full complement of cutesy plates in the university town of Burlington. So much for my theory.)

Earlier, in Jonestown, Pennsylvania, after we'd stopped at the Buck Inn to drink draft Yuengling and eat fresh fish with my wife's cousin, our teenager had grumbled from the backseat that we didn't have to drive this far to see rednecks. Of course I made her wash her mouth out with soap, but she was actually on to something. Although it's true that the whitetail-deer hunters and their girlfriends at the Buck had funny accents, the music on the jukebox and the humor at the bar were pretty much what you'd find in taverns from Southside Virginia to Texas. I didn't meet Snake and Outlaw (they were moving too fast), but I presume that they're the spiritual—maybe the literal—

descendants of the rednecks who constituted themselves the Green Mountain Boys and pulled off an operation at Ticonderoga that John Mosby wouldn't have been ashamed of.

A Hank Williams Jr. song on the Buck's jukebox reminded us that country boys come from "little towns all across this land." And from Pennsylvania to Vermont, small-town GAR monuments reminded us that these particular country boys, with their cousins from Ohio and Michigan, kicked Confederate butt in the early 1860s so effectively that one observer remarked that if he had Confederate cavalry and Union infantry he could whip any army on earth. To judge from the number of rebel flags I spotted on pickups and T-shirts, though, some of them won't make the same mistake next time. (By the way, the flag is incorporated in the sign for the Fields Tavern in Lorain County, Ohio, not far from Cleveland. When I passed by one September day, the Reverend Ed Wojnakowski was preaching at the "Independent Fundamental Baptist" church next door.)

North or South, Hank Jr.'s country boy is the small-town or rural version—sometimes found as a first- or second-generation migrant to some city, too—of the American "high prole" that Paul Fussell described in his book *Class*. These men have their skills; consequently "they have pride and a conviction of independence, and they feel some contempt for those who have not made it as far as they have." They also feel some contempt for the middle class. As one said to Fussell: "If my boy wants to wear a goddamn necktie all his life and bow and scrape to some boss, that's his right, but by God he should also have the right to earn an honest living with his hands if that is what he likes." Fussell argues that high proles have much in common with aristocrats besides scorn for the bourgeoisie. He cites their lack of concern with social climbing, their unromantic attitudes toward women, "their devotion to gambling and their fondness for deer hunting," and, in general, their tendency to make games and sports the central concern of their lives.

Be that as it may, V. S. Naipaul was certainly taken with the breed when he encountered it in his travels, described in *A Turn in the South*. A Mississippi informant helped him "see pride and style and a fashion code where I had seen nothing, made me notice what so far I hadn't sufficiently noticed: the pickup trucks dashingly driven, the baseball caps marked with the name of some company."

At the end, Naipaul gets downright lyrical about this "tribe, almost an Indian tribe, wandering freely over empty spaces," a view, he says, that "gave new poetry to what one saw on the highway."

Naipaul actually has a point (although it's tempting to make fun of him), but it won't do to romanticize these guys. They can be belligerent, sometimes for cause—and nothing makes them more belligerent than condescension—and sometimes just for the hell of it. Still, if there's going to be a fight, you want them on your side. And it may be that, as a recent, belligerent Charlie Daniels song has it, "What We Need Is a Few More Rednecks"—that is, "a little more respect / for the Lord and the law and the working man."

I'm writing this from California, just arrived, and I'm still on the lookout for the West Coast version. Our very first morning in the state, coming west from Nevada, we stopped for breakfast in Davis. As trucks loaded with tomatoes rumbled by outside, we eavesdropped on a conversation between two working men in the next booth. The one with the tattoos was saying that he used to be afraid of marriage because it was such a permanent commitment, but now that he realizes that it's not permanent he isn't afraid of it anymore. Later, his buddy urged him to take some time to go fishing and get in touch with himself. I don't know about this.

Motel California

Folks keep asking me when I'm going to write about California. They generally lick their chops when they ask it. They seem to think I'm going to trash the place. I wonder why? Anyway, yeah, it's true that I lived in the Golden State for almost a year recently, and I haven't said much about it. There's a reason for that.

You see, I went there intending just to lie low, do my work, and try to be unobtrusive. I took up volleyball and even bought some Birkenstock sandals (what my North Carolina students call "Air Jesus"). I resolved to keep an open mind and a closed mouth. Guests don't criticize their hosts. It's only polite. But Californians kept asking what I thought about their state, and my saying that I hadn't been there long enough to have an opinion usually wouldn't do. These

folks like their state a lot—those in the Bay Area, especially, love it
where they are—and they want to hear you agree with them.

Well, no Southerner should criticize folks for liking their state. It's
right that Californians should like California. But elsewhere people
don't always expect or even want outsiders to agree with them. Your
average New Yorker, for instance, couldn't care less whether you like
his state; in fact, if he thinks you're complaining about it, he'll try to
top you with some horror story of his own. Southerners do get angry
at outsiders' criticism, but we tend to believe you can't expect much
else from Yankees. Besides, without ignorant criticism to defend the
South against, being a Southerner wouldn't be half so much fun.

Anyway, when Californians insisted that I tell them what I thought,
sometimes I could get off the hook by raving about the restaurants,
the climate, and the scenery—all of which are truly wonderful. But
I don't like to lie outright, so when someone asked me point-blank
about the people and their folkways, I had to tell them that I found
California a strange place. I told enough of them that I might as well
tell you, too. Besides, now I'm safely back home.

Don't get me wrong. California has no monopoly on strangeness,
and anyway I have nothing against strangeness, as such. But California is strange in what are to me strange ways. Almost every day
brought some bizarre new observation: an aged coot roller-skating
in the shopping mall, a photograph in the *Stanford Daily* of a coed
shower in a Stanford residence hall, a flying squad of San Jose evangelists trying to exorcise San Francisco on Halloween, Ron Dellums's
political opinions being taken seriously—I could go on and on.

What really let me know I was in a different culture, though, was
that my otherwise normal California friends didn't find these things
remarkable. It wasn't that they'd lost their capacity for wonder or
shock—I could produce either with stories about the South. It's just
that my friends and I are *used to* different things.

Beyond that, it strikes me that there really are differences in what
we could call regional character. It's hard to write about this without
gross generalizing. (Sure, there are all kinds of exceptions, and I may
be wrong, anyway. I was only there for a year, after all.) It's also
hard to write about this without taking cheap shots. I mean, going to
California and complaining about rootlessness and narcissism is like
going to England and complaining about the food and the weather.

But that's what I noticed, and it's not just me. R. W. B. Lewis tells about William James's impressions of the Bay Area, when he went there in 1906 (just in time for the great earthquake, which impressed him considerably). James was getting $5,000 for a short series of lectures at Stanford on, among other things, the moral equivalent of war, and he had every reason to be happy. Like me, he found the climate ideal and the landscape stunning. In fact, Professor Lewis reports, James found everything pleasing, except the "social insipidity" and the "terrible 'historic vacuum and silence.'"

Now, I don't share James's stern New England view of insipidity (we Southerners do our best to be pleasant, too), but I do know what he meant. California is, after all, a state where "judgmental" is a bad word. My buddy Don, visiting from Michigan, joked that the license plates ought to say "I'm OK, You're OK." (New York plates, he suggested, could say "I'm OK, You Can Go F— Yourself.") I never actually heard the word *mellow,* but those Doonesbury cartoons a few years ago were right on the money.

Take the way Californians deal with hostility. It's not what I'm used to. Where a Southerner would respond with either frosty politeness or counter-hostility, a Californian may want to help you *work through* it. In any case, the object of your hostility is likely to see it as *your* problem. What this means is that hostility does no good at all. It doesn't even make you feel better.

In any case, and for whatever reason, give credit where it's due: the level of civility in casual public interaction is the highest I've ever experienced outside the South. It's remarkable how seldom you hear voices raised in anger, at least at strangers, in public—at other drivers, say. When you do, it's likely to be some out-of-stater who doesn't care about bad karma.

James's "historic vacuum and silence" is real enough, too. Any building from before the First World War is ancient. When images of the mythic past turn up (in advertising, say) they're from the Gold Rush days. The Spanish era seems to survive only in place-names, their original meanings long since forgotten. How else to explain "Los Altos Hills" or "Lake Lagunita"? Who seriously thinks of Our Lady of the Angels in connection with L.A., or of Santa Cruz as having anything to do with the cross of Christ?

The result, for some of us anyway, is reflected in one of my favorite California stories. When some professor (I believe it was

Hugh Kenner) who had taught there for many years left to take a job back east, someone asked him how it felt to be leaving after all that time. "Like checking out of a motel," he said.

California, what I saw of it, is like that: very pleasant, a good place to spend some time, but not somewhere you could actually get attached to. I have fond memories, but I don't *miss* it, exactly—not like I missed the South. Most Californians seem to feel the same way; in fact, many don't even recognize that there's any other way to feel. They came to California in the first place because they liked what it had to offer; if somewhere else offers more, they'll move on (as many now seem to be doing to Oregon and, God help us, North Carolina). Location is just another consumer decision, a utilitarian, cost-benefit calculation—a different proposition from liking a place because it's your home. When Californians ask you to admire their state, they're asking you to compliment their discernment and good taste, just as they'd like you to admire their choice of automobile or wine.

Some people have argued that the South is the most American part of America—usually as a compliment, though sometimes (as in a trashy book called *The Southern Mystique*) not. But John Crowe Ransom claimed in *I'll Take My Stand* that, no, the South is the most *European* part of the nation. I now think Ransom was right. The South is different from the rest of the country, and especially from California, in many of the same ways Europe is different from America as a whole.

Two of my friends in California were Englishmen. Both grew up loving American music (jazz for one, rock and roll for the other); both came to the United States straight out of university, became citizens, and haven't looked back. Both love America. Both told me, in almost exactly the same words, "If you like America, you should like California."

I can see that. It's as easy for a Southerner to make fun of California as a sort of New Age Florida as it is for Europeans to make fun of bumptious, naive, self-absorbed America. But California can be exhilarating. The liberation from the past, from attachment to a social and even physical "place," the freedom to pursue happiness any way you can afford, the sheer newness and flux and sense of unending *possibility*—that's what America used to offer, and California still does. And that can be powerfully alluring, particularly to someone unhappy with a more rigid or traditional place—a place, that is, like England, or the South.

Yeah, I can see it. But it doesn't appeal to me. Frankly, I feel about California the way some of my Baptist friends feel about Bob Jones University, that it's a caricature of their tradition, an exaggeration of some of its features to the point of ugliness. No doubt if California were a separate country, I'd find its culture as charmingly exotic as its landscape and cuisine. But I don't like the idea that one American congressman in eight comes from there: those guys make laws that I have to obey. I don't like being held responsible as an American for what Californians do (no more, I presume, than they like being held accountable for what Southerners do). Most of all, though, I don't like being made to feel like the kind of anti-American European I've always despised.

Cardinal Sins

After sharing my ill-informed impressions of California with you in the last piece, I should probably just let it be. After all, only fools think they understand the South after a few months, and I presume the same is true for California. Besides, lots of people have been to the Bay Area. Some even live there.

But they're not writing this. And expatriation in the Spandex State seems to have dried me up on the subject of the South. I just don't feel back *in touch* yet. So for now it looks as if it's California or nothing—and, no, I'm not putting it to a vote. Tell you what: I'll just tell a few stories and go easy on the meaning of it all.

In the let's-be-fair department, let me praise the scenery. The San Francisco Bay really is as beautiful as everybody says. I'm a pushover for the combination of steep hills and big water, and the fog is a definite asset, rolling in and out of the Golden Gate like God's own lava lamp, endlessly diverting. Every prospect pleases.

But I must say that I kept running into people who made me want to go out and find a baby seal to club. This was especially true in Marin County, where BMWs and New Age thought seem to coexist comfortably. All I can say is that Cyra McFadden wasn't far off the mark in *The Serial*—which, if you haven't read it, you should, if only for the character who is regarded as an intellectual because she has two M.A.'s: one in sociology and one in macrame.

Across the bay in Berkeley, the graffiti were a healthier mix than they used to be; one Maoist poster, for instance, had been defaced with "666" on Mao's forehead. But the notorious People's Park has become an encampment for the deranged, the drug-addled, and the just plain shiftless, a depot for human debris swept westward by less tolerant communities to a place where there really is a free lunch, and supper, too. Berkeley being what it is, these vagrants were politically organized, demanding what they were urged to think of as their rights from a community they seemed to have thoroughly buffaloed. As somebody once observed, there's nothing wrong with liberal guilt, but they always seem to feel guilty about the wrong things.

Of course, California has been strange for a long time, as a great Berkeley house reminded us. The former "Temple of the Wing" [*sic*] was originally built without walls, a sort of colonnaded platform on which folks lived and, I gather, ate nuts and berries. It has walls now, but it still commands a marvelous view of the Bay, and the ghost of Isadora Duncan haunts the place. The same architect did the University of California faculty club building, a splendid Aztec-Oriental hunting-lodge affair. A while back there was a movement to remove the mounted animal heads that decorate the dining room on grounds of antispeciesism or some such twaddle, but common sense prevailed for once.

Most of my impressions are not of Berkeley, however, but of Stanford. We lived for the year on that university's campus, in a charming little adobe hacienda built by Mrs. Herbert Hoover for impecunious junior faculty, and now worth roughly a quarter-million dollars in the "depressed" California real-estate market. Folks at Stanford were very gracious to us, and I don't want to pick on the place. Besides, it has enough troubles already. Our year there saw revelations of how overhead money from federal research grants went for things like sheets for the president's custom-made bed. And you've probably read about this "political correctness" business, too. (Our nation's pack journalists should be penalized for piling on, by the way: where have they been all this time?) Anyway, I'll just say that everything you've heard on that subject is true, but I survived. I just dropped by the Hoover Institution from time to time to get my head straight.

No, Stanford's a great university, arguably the best one west of Fort Smith. Let's get that on the record. It has a first-rate faculty and smart students, and if you think humanistic learning there is not a pretty sight, just wait until what Stanford's doing trickles down to Generic State U. But it is a funny place.

One evening I was leaving the university library with Susan Howatch's book *Glamorous Powers* when the student at the check-out desk raised an eyebrow and asked if it was any good. Realizing that the title does sound a little Judith Krantz-y, I mumbled that the book is about the Church of England. The student asked if there was anything in it about monks. "I'm working on a paper on the cenobitic tradition," he said. Impressed that an undergraduate knew the meaning of "cenobitic," I told him there were some Anglican Benedictines in the book, but it was mostly about ecclesiastical politics—"sort of like Trollope, but around World War II."

"Trollope," the kid said. "Is that a writer?"

As I said, Stanford students are bright. They know a lot. But it's next to impossible to guess *what* they know, especially now that Jesse Jackson's friends have cleansed the curriculum of works by dead white European males.

Another story. The dean of the Stanford chapel is an old friend from North Carolina, an Episcopal priest who used to teach at the Duke Divinity School. As you might guess, he wasn't terribly sound to start with, but California hasn't been good for him. On the first Sunday in Advent, for instance, music for the chapel services was provided by a (first-rate) jazz guitarist who played "Someday My Prince Will Come." At other services we found ourselves praying alternately to God the Father and God the Mother. Now, I don't know how you feel about it, but that strikes me as rather *Hindu.* I mean, I can live with a genderless deity, but a hermaphroditic one gives me the creeps. Anyway, these, ah, manifestations are locked into rather traditional sex-roles. The father gets to do all the whiz-bang creating, for instance, and the mother seems to be into nurturing. Maybe they mix it up on alternate Sundays and I just missed it. Neither parent makes any *judgments,* of course.

Speaking of which, while we were there Stanford announced a new "domestic partners" policy that opened married student housing to unmarried couples—including unmarried couples of the same sex.

When there was an outcry from some married students, my buddy the dean of the chapel chaired a "town meeting" to discuss the new policy. The principal opposition came from foreign students who didn't want their children exposed to American ways—at least not these American ways. Asians (the p.c. word for Orientals) seemed especially inclined to this sort of judgmental insensitivity, but what brought the meeting to an abrupt and noisy end was the observation by a Muslim student that in his country, of course, it would be his duty to kill homosexuals.

Has anyone really thought through this business of "multiculturalism"?

Anyway, on the ground, outside the hothouse of the university, multiculturalism is a working daily reality in the Bay Area. UHF television offers programs in Spanish, Japanese, Farsi, Italian, Evangelical—name your group, and the liability lawyers and chiropractors are advertising in their language.

This has done great things for the restaurant scene. We ate out most nights: Chinese, of course (some from provinces I'd never even heard of), Mexican (the real thing, still rare in these parts, where "Mexican" means either Taco Bell or a place modeled after one in Vail where the radiologist-owner goes to ski); Japanese (at what was said to be the best sushi bar in San Francisco—and I *still* didn't like it); gay (at a hamburger joint called "Hot and Hunky"). . . . Thai, Korean, and Vietnamese we can get around here (those cuisines are as common as Big Macs in Fayetteville, home of Fort Bragg and innumerable war brides and camp followers), so we slighted them for food from places where the Airborne hasn't been yet: North and South Indian, Persian, Indonesian, Burmese, and Ethiopian.

My buddy Sam said once (we were eating in an Afghan restaurant in D.C. at the time) that whenever a Third World country fell to the Communists a new cuisine bloomed in Washington. In the Bay Area the same refugees have faced stiffer competition and a more discerning clientele, and the results are definitely worth writing home about.

We even went to the mother church of "California cuisine," Chez Panisse in Berkeley. I wanted to check out the original of what every mesquite-grilled monkfish with kiwi fruit and goat cheese fern-bar in piedmont North Carolina is imitating. I figured not going would be like avoiding ribs in Memphis, crawfish in New Orleans, or barbecue in Goldsboro, so I did my duty—and enjoyed it. It seems I only break out in hives when I run into the same thing in Raleigh. You know, there's no reason California shouldn't have its own cuisine, and I don't think I'd mind it even in Raleigh if it were plainly just another kind of foreign restaurant. After all, I like Thai food in Fayetteville partly because it's exotic. The problem with the California stuff is that it won't *stay* exotic.

Anyway, now even a suburb like Mountain View offers an amazing variety of cuisines. Walking the main street, we felt as if we were in some exotic entrepôt, a vestpocket version of Singapore, say, or Beirut (in the old days). This is not unpleasant, and certainly the new immigrants seem to do most of the actual *work* in those parts. In fact, if it weren't for Asians and Hispanics, it looks to me as if the economic base of the Bay Area would be a matter of bicycle and roller-skate shops.

By the way, I wrote "Hispanics" instead of "Mexicans" not just to be p.c. A friend whose wife teaches first grade in San Jose reported that more than half of her students were Latin American—not just Mexican, but Honduran, Nicaraguan, Salvadoran: differences I suspect most of us in the East never even think about. The same is true for "Asians," a culturally meaningless hodgepodge of a concept if there ever was one.

Much the same variety can be found within the *voluntary* subcultures. Whatever your hobby, enthusiasm, political or sexual kink, you can find others who share it and gather to do it or talk about it—Tocqueville gone berserk. Some folks go to church on Sunday morning? That's cool. Up the road a ways, at the same hour, a hundred motorcyclists gather at Alice's Restaurant for brunch. Off in the other direction, a group of software engineers, aging hippies, and lesbian potters get together to sing the old Primitive Baptist shapenote music. There are weekend subcultures of witches, nudists, and skateboarders—each with its own computer bulletin board.

Those, like me, whose development was arrested in the fifties can listen to KOFY, 1050 AM, a radio station that plays only songs from that era. (One listener called in to say that his twenty-year-younger wife loves the music he grew up with and "it turns her on in the most delicious way.") They can drive around in fender-skirted '57 Chevies with bumper stickers that say "The Heartbeat of America—Yesterday's Chevrolet," and they can go to Saturday-morning gatherings of other enthusiasts. On Saturday night, they can swing by the Peninsula Creamery for a chocolate malt; only the prices have changed since 1958 (but, boy, have they ever). They can dance the night away at ShBoom, a club in San Jose that plays only old rock and roll. Or they can stay home and watch Channel 20's *Dance Party,* sort of an *American Bandstand* for the dental-floss set, where people our age put on their old letter sweaters and poodle skirts and show the youngsters how it ought to be done. And this is *Northern California.*

This is partly an urban thing, of course. Georg Simmel wrote about it. It also requires general levels of affluence and leisure that once belonged exclusively to an aristocracy. Tom Wolfe has written about that. But there's a California overlay on all of this, an ethic of hedonism and tolerance, coupled with an almost complete absence of noblesse oblige. I'll let you draw your own conclusions about whether this is wholesome libertarianism or a breakdown in society's immune system (if you'll excuse the metaphor), but it is something like what Robert Bellah and his colleagues wrote about in *Habits of the Heart.* That book once troubled me because it didn't describe any America *I* knew, but now I see where it's coming from—literally. These California professors did a survey in the Bay Area and thought they were talking about America. Well, they weren't. Not yet, anyway.

Guess I got into the meaning of it all, after all, didn't I? Sorry about that. I'm glad to be home.

A Good Job for the Federales

There is good reason to be suspicious of the national park system. You can start with its origins.

In 1864, an act of Congress seized the first park land for the federal government, evicting some homesteaders from the Yosemite Valley and directing the State of California to administer the place. In the context of the Civil War, maybe one more little bit of federal usurpation hardly mattered, but things went downhill from there. Barely twenty-five years later, the feds decided they didn't like the way California was running things and grabbed Yosemite for themselves.

That they did this at the urging of John Muir, sappy Scottish pantheist and the original California flake, is another reason to be suspicious. Muir had little faith in omnipotent deity, but a lot in omnipotent government: God had preserved the trees so far, he wrote, but "only Uncle Sam" could save them now. As you might suppose, Muir admired Thoreau and Emerson, and maybe someone can explain to me sometime why New England individualism—even when transplanted to California by a Scot—always seems to lead to expanded federal power.

Anyway, as a promotional movie about Yosemite says, with no trace of embarrassment or irony, "the [federal] parks were our first massively endowed works of art," and, of course, if it comes to a choice between Yosemite and *Piss Christ,* there's no question which side I'm on. Still, it was with a jaundiced eye and a readiness to be unimpressed that I drove from the Bay Area up through the California gold country. Yosemite was expecting three million visitors that year, and my wife and I were off to be two of them.

It was dark when we got there, so we didn't see much on the way in. Most of our fellow tourists at the lodge were giving off hearty emanations of the backpacking sort, so much so that I was secretly pleased when the young couple ahead of me at the store bought a carton of Camels, a six-pack of King Cobra malt liquor, and a pint of peppermint schnapps. Party time.

Given my political and cultural misgivings (to get to the point), you can imagine my surprise the next morning when I was completely captivated by the place.

There's more to it than natural beauty, although of course the place is beautiful, especially with snow still on the peaks and the waterfalls at full freshet. But I've seen beautiful: Greek islands, Cornish cliffs, Italian lakes, Javanese volcanos, fern jungles in Jamaica, rice paddies in Orissa. . . . I can place-drop with the best of them. Yosemite, though—well, it *moved* me, in a way these other gorgeous places never did. I came away puzzled about that, but ready to ignore my anti-statist principles if that's what it takes to keep college boys from painting their fraternities' letters on El Capitan, or some Trumpoid developer from building a gated resort that we common folk can't visit.

A couple of months later, these heretical thoughts were reinforced at the Grand Canyon, which we visited on our way back to North Carolina. We'd driven from Palo Alto down to Bakersfield, where the

music on the radio, the accents in the filling stations, and the general
seediness of the roadscape made me feel right at home. I regretted
that we didn't have time to stop for an Okie Girl beer, or a prayer
meeting at a roadside tabernacle, but we pressed on past borax works
and joshua trees into Arizona.

Now, when it comes to desert scenery, I'm afraid I'm pretty much
tone-deaf. Most of what we were driving through looked to me like
West Virginia after the strip miners got through with it, and as we
approached the Canyon I was ready with observations like "This
would take care of our landfill needs for a century." Once again,
though, I was confounded by a remarkable *place*. In the event I
sounded like Richard Nixon at the Great Wall: "This really is a . . .
grand . . . canyon." I didn't find it beautiful, exactly; in fact, it was
sort of appalling. But it was moving in much the same way Yosemite
had been.

Later, driving across Kansas, I had a lot of time to think about
this. What was it about these places that knocked the smart-aleck
right out of me?

It wasn't the "wilderness" angle. From time to time as a teenage
spelunker I stood where I was certain no one had ever stood before,
and, sure, it was a kick. But this was a different, more subtle thrill.

I remembered the year we lived in Jerusalem, and the time we took
a visiting friend, an American Protestant, to the Holy Sepulchre. She
was almost literally sickened by the incense and candles and images,
by the Italian Franciscans gliding about, the creepy-looking Greeks
and sinister Armenians, not to mention the shabby Copts and Syrian
Jacobites, and the ragged Ethiopians in their mud huts on the roof.
None of this had much to do with her image of the hill far away
where the old rugged cross stood, and she was relieved to discover
"Gordon's Calvary" and the so-called Garden Tomb, located in a
quiet, sunny park outside the Old City's walls. These spots have
nothing to do with Good Friday and Easter ("Chinese" Gordon's
crack-brain theories notwithstanding), but she found them "much
more like it was, don't you think?"

Well, yeah. But I prefer the traditional sites. Even if they aren't
where Christ died and was buried, they are holy places. Centuries
of piety have made them that. Just so, I realized, for me the appeal
of Yosemite and the Canyon lies largely in the fact that so many

have stood there before. What charmed me most about those ancient rocks and rivers was their quite recent past, the fossil evidence of excursion trains, tent villages, and pseudo-Indian lodges, reminders of tourism in the Age of Steam. What moved me was the thought of Teddy Roosevelt and the ubiquitous Frederick Law Olmsted and old John Muir and all the others who had marveled at the same sights I was seeing.

In a sense, even I had been there before. Those vistas were almost clichés, familiar from postcards and home movies and my boyhood stamp collection. When I saw Yosemite's Mirror Lake—now Mirror Marsh, inexorably on the way to becoming Mirror Meadow—I thought, damn it, that's not *right.* That's not what the stereopticon slide looks like. That's not what Teddy Roosevelt saw. Let's get in the Corps of Engineers and *dredge* that sucker!

No, virgin wilderness may have its charms, but give me a worldly old courtesan of a place, where I can think about those who've been there before me. Given my choice of mighty redwoods, I'll take the one people used to drive Model T's through.

You know, it's funny, but going to the Grand Canyon and Yosemite made me feel like an American, just as visiting the Holy Sepulchre made me feel like a Christian—part of a tradition. Caressed by a hundred million eyes, mere natural wonders have acquired a patina; they've become national icons, part of our cultural patrimony. My libertarian friends may disagree, but it seems to me that maintaining these secular holy places is a pretty good thing for the federal government to do.

Home Movies

The first day of our journey back home to North Carolina after a year in California took us past Bakersfield, where I'm told the children and grandchildren of Okies have imposed something resembling Southern culture on a part of California, and I'm sorry we didn't have more time to check it out. Back here in Tarheelia, alas, something resembling California culture is being imposed on a part of Dixie. Anyway, after that, our trip essentially retraced the Okies' route from the Dust Bowl, in reverse. Let me tell you about it. (Sorry I can't show you my slides.)

Crossing Arizona and New Mexico, we were going parallel to old Route 66, and sometimes we got off the Interstate to get our kicks on that famous highway, now bypassed. These days it's a lonesome drive, through a landscape of what we recognized from innumerable cowboy movies as buttes, mesas, gulches—stuff like that. There sure is a lot of landscape out yonder, and after a while it takes on a certain, shall we say, sameness. Whenever my attention flagged, though, I pictured a foreground of Okie jalopies headed slowly, wearily west, or broken down by the side of the road, radiators boiling over, a Woody Guthrie song on the soundtrack. All I can say is things must have been pretty dire in Oklahoma.

At intervals we saw reminders of Route 66's day as a main east-west artery: rusted signs, boarded-up gas stations, deserted snake and monkey farms, Indian trading posts back once again to serving only Indians. It was fun to picture summer after summer's worth of children arguing over where the *exact* middles of backseats were, back when travel was still slow enough to be something other than just a way to a destination.

Highway travel in the Southwest is still a bargain, or so it seemed after a year in the high-priced part of California. The food was mostly just good, greasy grub, but I'd already filled my sushi and cilantro quotas for the next twenty years anyway. Decent motels ran $20 to $30 a night, and in Holbrook, Arizona, gateway to the Petrified Forest (and ain't *that* something?), we stopped at one, the Wigwam Motel. The Wigwam is a splendid period piece that ought to be on the National Register, but only three of its tepee-shaped cabins were occupied the night we were there. Give it a try if you're in the neighborhood, or at least give it a tomahawk chop as you pass by.

Unlike many other "American-owned" motels we saw, the Wigwam doesn't advertise that fact on its sign. Most of the other places we stayed were run by what my wife and I have come to call, generically, "Patels," because it seems that most of the Gujaratis who run small motels in the United States do in fact have that surname. (Have you noticed? What is this, some kind of inn-keeping caste?) I'm sorry to see them run afoul of nativism, if that's what's happening, because it seems to me that *they're* real Americans, maybe the last: hard-working, thrifty, family-oriented. And whatever may be going on in big cities, it seems to me that Asian immigrants to small towns are assimilating quickly. Already some of the Asian students at my university are more Southern in accent and style than faculty kids who grew up in Chapel Hill. And it's not surprising: they're the children of doctors or restauranteurs or motel-keepers from small North Carolina towns, probably the only Asian graduates of their high schools. Probably honors graduates, too, bless 'em.

Anyway, there's a lot of *there* there in small-town and rural Arizona and New Mexico. We saw places less like North Carolina than any other part of the United States I know, places different from here in ways different from other places that are different from here, if you follow that.

But that can't be said of Santa Fe. When we detoured there briefly to see friends it felt as if we'd somehow warped back into California. Thanks to rigorous zoning, Santa Fe does have a distinctive look, a sort of Walt Disney Adobe-land effect. But most of those adobes have been built in the last fifty years, and increasingly, I'm told, Santa Fe is becoming part of exurban Los Angeles, home to very rich folks who commute now and then by private plane.

Why (I asked my friend) have all these Californians moved to New Mexico? I mean, you can find pseudo-Spanish architecture a lot closer to Beverly Hills.

"You don't understand," he said. "These are the ones who think they're artists."

And of course the coin dropped. Santa Fe is Carmel-in-the-desert. Or Sodom-in-the-desert (we heard about one woman's intimate relations with a tiger-trainer, and subsequently, it was rumored, with his tiger). Anyway, these are the pseud rich, who dabble in art, drugs, and kinky sex—not the philistine rich, who dabble in golf, alcohol, and mere adultery. Poor folks like Mexican construction workers or Indian jewelry-makers or tutors at St. John's College must live in housetrailers on some windswept patch of scrub 'way out of town.

What's wrong with Santa Fe is exemplified by the merchants who were lobbying against street vendors, arguing that grubby Indians sitting on the sidewalk peddling jewelry (at prices lower than those in the stores) soil the "Rodeo Drive–style merchandising environment" that they have created. I take some pleasure from the thought that those Indians were sitting there long before anyone spoke English in Santa Fe and will probably be there long after the last English-speaker is gone.

One place they sit is in front of the old governor's palace, now a museum where we took in an exhibit on New Mexico's short Civil War history, which began when a force of Texans swarmed up the Rio Grande with the cry "On to San Francisco!" I must say that their plan to capture California's gold and unblockaded ports strikes me as awfully ambitious. I'd just driven from the Bay Area and knew in my posterior how far away it is. Still, the campaign did begin well, with a victory over the Colorado Volunteers at Valverde.

I didn't realize the present hostility between Texans and Coloradans went back so far, but at Valverde a Colorado officer rallied his troops with the cry "They're Texans, boys! Give 'em hell!" It didn't work, though, and the rebs raised their flag over Santa Fe on March 5, 1862, before losing a battle, and the campaign, at Glorieta. (A long retreat through the desert back to Texas cost more lives than combat had: 500 of the 3,700 Confederate troops were battle casualties; 1,200 died from "other" causes.) The exhibit in Santa Fe displayed wedding rings found in a recently opened mass Confederate grave at Glorieta and informed us that high-tech methods matching bone samples with tissue from known descendants make it likely that the bones will be identified and returned to Texas for burial.

Anyway, after the glitz of Santa Fe we went on, with some relief, to Las Vegas, New Mexico, sixty miles up the Santa Fe trail and not glitzy in the least—in fact, a little on the down-at-the-heels side. Las Vegas had its high point when the railroad came through in the late nineteenth century, as dozens of once splendid houses attest, and there you can see what is left of a real wild West town (where outlaws were hanged by the score from the local windmill) with little subsequent overlay and apparently little hope of attracting the tourist trade. Aside from an endless motorcade through town for a returning Desert Storm veteran, nothing much was happening in Las Vegas. It looked as if nothing much had happened for a long time.

From Las Vegas to Tucumcari is 106 miles, and we counted every single one because we made the mistake of beginning with only a quarter-tank of gas. The New Mexico highlands are beautiful, in a desolate sort of way, and they were damn near deserted. In the entire stretch we saw only six other cars and one gas station (and it was closed). We passed gates opening on dirt roads leading to out-of-sight ranch houses; one sign said "House 16 miles." But we made it to Tucumcari, refueled, and drove northeast to Dalhart, Texas, a charmless place surrounded by cattle feedlots and right aromatic when the wind is right, which it was. The natives were friendly, though, in what seemed a Texas sort of way—or was I imagining things? Anyway, after a whole year in California without going near a hot tub I figured it was all right now that I was back in the Old Confederacy, so I soaked the travel off of me at the Super 8 Motel. Felt good, too.

The next morning found us in the town of Guymon, capital of a patch of ground known as "No Man's Land" because at one time neither Texas nor Oklahoma claimed it. Oklahoma blinked first, and got it. Guymon was the heart of the Dust Bowl, and I thought once again of the Okies and their Great Trek. It's a hell of a trip even now, in an air-conditioned Plymouth Voyager. We soon crossed into Kansas, arriving at the town of Liberal, proud home of both the Shrove Tuesday Pancake Race and "Oztoberfest," where people dress up like characters from the Oz books. Somehow we knew we'd reached the Midwest.

The next day we explored the ruins of Kansas City, a grand early-twentieth-century American city, lingering at its splendid Great War memorial and museum, dedicated by General Pershing and Marshall Foch when we thought war had been ended, but now rather odd in its attention to that unmemorable conflict. Kansas City's best days may be behind it, but it is still a famous barbecue town, and I was perplexed to eat barbecue as good as I've ever had—in a place that was all wrong.

KC Masterpiece is a restaurant, definitely not a *joint,* located in a suburban shopping center and owned by an M.D. It sells its sauce in supermarkets nationwide, serves Buffalo chicken wings and Monterey salad, and violates nearly all of my buddy Vince Staten's rules for good barbecue. (For instance: a good place has flies. If there are no flies, you should ask what the flies know that you don't.) But, my, it was good. That supermarket sauce is real good (try it), but the meat was memorable. My beef brisket was merely wonderful, but my wife's pork tenderloin was sublime. She wouldn't trade me nearly enough of it. The next day we went to Arthur

Bryant's, over by the old ballpark, a barbecue mecca ever since Calvin Trillin wrote it up. Its atmosphere is 100 percent correct, and it is a great joint with fine pork barbecue—but it's not as good as KC Masterpiece.

From KC onwards, the trip got less exotic as we went on through Missouri to North Carolina, via Ohio (don't ask), so I'll cut this short. What I want to know, though, is this: how can anyone travel this continent and believe that regional differences are unimportant? Shoot, my distant kinsman Peter Taylor wrote a whole novel *(Summons to Memphis)* and John Hiatt a great song ("Memphis in the Meantime") about the difference between Nashville and Memphis. You want to talk about Holbrook, or Dalhart, or Liberal? Good Lord. No, America only looks uniform when viewed from far away—from the coasts, or from 30,000 feet in the air. Up close, it remains a delightful hodgepodge.

Fight Them on the Beaches

Before I drove from California to North Carolina, I believed that U.S. regionalism was alive and well. Now I damn well know it is. I'll tell you what I *am* worried about, though, is England.

Recently my wife and I flew direct from Charlotte to London. That possibility didn't exist until recently, and I'm not sure it's a good thing for either Charlotte or London that it does now. At the least, it's disconcerting to go direct from Billy Graham Boulevard to Victoria Station without depressurizing. Changing airports in New York really ought to be part of European travel, don't you think?

Anyway, finding ourselves back in London for the first time in a dozen years (having missed the entire Thatcher era), we were struck by how much less *English* the place seems these days. We'd no sooner entered the Underground than we were looking at a big poster showing a couple of guys sitting on a front porch in what was said to be Benson, North Carolina, drinking Budweiser. Now it's nice that Benson is still exotic enough to have some cachet, but I find it sinister that Budweiser is available at all in the country that taught me to like bitter and brown ale.

The real problem, though, is less creeping Americanization, that perennial bugbear of the English left (and much of the old Tory right), than it is galloping cosmopolitanism in general. For instance, speaking of brew, the museum cafeteria at the Victoria and Albert doesn't sell British beer at all, just the Dutch and German lagers that one of my English friends calls "Euro-fizz."

Worse, when I went into a Knightsbridge delicatessen and asked for Wensleydale cheese, the pleasant young Pakistani behind the counter looked puzzled. "Wensleydale," he said. "Doesn't ring a bell."

Same with clothing. The Harris tweed jackets I bought twelve years earlier having apparently shrunk around the middle, I went back to the same Oxford Street shop to buy one or two more, but all I found were double-breasted Italian numbers, with wide pointy lapels. When I asked the clerk (who was wearing one) if they had any clothes that don't make you look like a damn gigolo, he suggested, sneering, that I try "someplace that caters more to the tourist trade." (After smarting under that insult for a while, I did, and found what I was after.)

Even in matters of language some Brits seem determined to jettison their heritage. While we were there, an article in the *Telegraph* reported that BBC radio is going to read through the Bible, but despite the recommendation of the poetry department and listener mail that ran ten to one in favor of the King James Version, the religion department was holding out for a modern translation.

At least one tradition persists, however: the bloodymindedness of the English worker seems to have been unaffected by all the years of Thatcherism. Studying in the splendid old reading room of the British Museum one afternoon, for example, I was forcibly reminded that the ghost of Karl Marx haunts the place in more ways than one: the stillness was shattered by a great clearing of throat on a public address system I'd never realized was there, and a working-class voice announced that no more books would be delivered to readers that day because of "indoostrial action" by the library staff. (Scores of shabby scholars shuffled, grumbling, to the exits.)

Outside of London it was easier to believe that maybe, just maybe, there will always be an England. Where else, for instance, would people eat strawberries and Devonshire cream on the lawn of a grand country house (in our case, Cliveden, Lady Astor's estate on the Thames), then sit in the rain to watch an amateur production of *The*

Taming of the Shrew? And where else would there be a market for something called a "chip butty": french fries on white bread, with mayonnaise?

And, despite all the incursions of unEnglish ways, many Englishfolk retain a strong, irreverent, xenophobic streak that I rather admire—at least when it's not surfacing as cruel and pointless Paki-bashing. Consider the following unattributed verse, protesting the Channel Tunnel linking Great Britain to the Continent. (It was passed on to me by a friend who copied a copy of a copy, and it seems to be an example of modern, urban photocopy folklore, but if it has a known author I'd like to be corrected.)

Ode to the Chunnel

There'll be carloads of Louises
From Parisian stripteases
Importing foul diseases
Into Kent.

There'll be modern French Wells-Fargoes
Sending juggernauts with cargoes
Of froglegs and escargots
And men's scent.

There'll be Dutchmen, too, by jingo,
Who'll refuse to speak the lingo,
Coming over for the bingo
And the dogs.

And through this umbilical,
Seeking knickers from St. Michael,
Girls from Rotterdam will cycle
In their clogs.

There'll be Danes on every corner,
Faces pink after a sauna,
Trying hard to sell us porno-
Graphic books.

There'll be men like Julius Caesar
Getting in without a visa,
Careless architects from Pisa,
Bloody crooks.

There'll be wealthy German campers
With enormous picnic hampers
Full of sauerkraut and champers
And pork pies.

There'll be Eyeties slick and smarmy,
Reared on pizza and salami,
Turning up at Veeraswamy
Without ties.

There'll be Swedes of charmless candour
Coming over to philander
Spreading left-wing propaganda
Against wealth.

Belgian girls of great proportions
Who have failed to take precautions
Will drive over for abortions
On the Health.

There'll be Spanish señoritas
Jamming all our parking meters
With their miserable pesetas—
I don't know!

And señors doing sambas
Shouting "*Vamos!*" and "*Caramba!*"
And believing that the amber
Light means "go".

There'll be Austrians with poodles
Wanting membership of Boodles,
Then demanding apple strudels
With their tea.

There'll be lecherous Kuwaitis
Driving lorryloads of Katies
From the Thames to the Euphrates,
C.O.D.

There'll be men from Lithuania,
From Rumania and Albania,
Pennsylvania and Tasmania,
I've no doubt.

So, dear immigration panel,
Boys in sports jackets and flannel,
Please protect our English Channel—
Keep them out!

Now *that's* the England I remember, and one thing I liked about it was that it wasn't sure it liked *me*.

VI
Covering Dixie like Kudzu

Shall We Gather by the River?

When I was invited to be a judge at the 1992 Memphis in May World Championship Barbecue Cooking Contest some envious backbiters put it about that it wasn't because I'm well known as a discriminating ami de swine, but because my sister knows the woman who picks the judges. I have just one thing to say to them.

Eat your heart out.

Naturally I jumped on the chance like a dog on a—well, on a rib bone. The annual Memphis contest offers not just some of the best 'cue in the world but a complete barbecultural experience. I heard that the 1991 festival, for instance, drew entire platoons of Elvis impersonators, not to mention a contestant billing himself as "M. C. Hamhock" who promoted his product with a rap jingle:

> Don't need no knife, don't need no fork,
> Just wrap your lips around my pork.

So it was that I found myself winging over to Memphis one lovely Friday in May, eating American Airlines' peanuts and reading their copy of *Entertainment Weekly*, where I found a record review that began: "For many music fans north of the Mason-Dixon line, contemporary white Southern culture is nothing but an *Easy Rider* cliché of booze, bikes, and bad attitude." Yeeee-haw! Pig—sooey!

On the ground in Memphis, my sister and I walked down Beale Street toward the riverside park where the contest was being held, past the usual street vendors offering assorted Afro-schlock and Deadhead tie-dye. When we came to one selling plastic pig-snouts we knew we were getting close. Soon the unmistakable smell of hickory smoke assailed us and we rounded a bend into the park to behold 180-odd tents, booths, pavilions, kiosks, huts, gazebos, and God knows what all else stretched out before us, literally on the riverbank, just a few feet from the mighty Mississippi. It was an amazing sight, its surreality heightened by daredevil youths bungee-jumping from a crane on the bluff above us and by the tract I was given as I entered the park, a handy guide to "What to Do in Case You Miss the Rapture." (Just a tip: if you take any marks or prints on your forehead or hands you'll be sorry.)

In the park we wandered about, gaping. Some mom-and-pop operations had made do with folding lawn chairs and simple funeral-home tents, but other teams had assembled two- and three-story structures with latticework, decks, statuary, and hanging plants. Each team had a name (something about barbecue seems to provoke bad puns) and many also had mottoes, like "Hogs smell better barbecued" and "We serve no swine before it's time." Portable generators powered everything from electric fans to fountains to neon signs; over their drone mighty sound systems pumped out music, mostly country, Cajun, or rap, but I also caught the strains of the Village People's "YMCA."

Each team had a smoking apparatus, of course, and some had two or three. They ranged from backyard Weber pots to a tractor-trailer behemoth billed as the world's largest portable barbecue cooker, but most were roughly coffin-sized, some of them obviously off-the-rack, others pieced together from fifty-five-gallon drums and stovepipe. Any doubts that barbecue contests are serious business were dispelled by the trophies on display: some teams had more brass than the U.S. Army. And everywhere you looked you saw the pig-totem of the People of the Swine.

Now, for years I've kept a mental log of barbecue joint signs. I've seen pigs reclining, running, and dancing; pigs with bibs, with knives and forks, with crowns and scepters. I've seen pigs as beauty contest winners, pigs in Confederate uniforms, and pigs in cowboy hats (one with a banjo). I've seen Mr. and Mrs. Pig dressed for a night on the town, and Mr. and Mrs. Pig as American Gothic. But I never saw pigs like I saw in Memphis. Pigs in chefs' hats and volunteer firemen's helmets. A pig in a Memphis State football uniform triumphant over some University of Tennessee pigs. A pig in a Superman suit rising from the flames. A pig reclining in a skillet; another on a grill, drinking beer. Two pigs basting a little gnomish person on a spit, and (on the T-shirts of a team called the Rowdy Southern Swine) a whole trainload of partying pigs. It's a hard call, but my favorite was probably some pigs with wings and haloes, from a team called Hog Heaven.

Italy was being honored by the Festival, so a number of teams struck what they took to be Italian notes. (I gather that New Zealand, the honoree-nation the previous year, had inspired mostly tasteless sheep jokes.) Some sites were decorated with hanging bunches of plastic grapes or simulated marble columns, T-shirts said "Ciao Down," and there were almost as many Italian flags as Confederate ones. Of course the pig signs got into the act, too. Pigs ate pizza. Pigs wore handlebar mustaches. Pigs reclined in gondolas. Pigs stomped grapes. Pigs posed in gladiator gear and togas and Mafia outfits. A piece of doggerel posted in one booth combined the common themes of Italy, mortality, and beer:

Shall We Gather by the River?

> Arrivederci my pug-nosed pal
> We'll meet again at a different locale
> You in your mud, me drinking a Bud
> Way up in the final corral.

If any actual Italians were present to receive this hands-across-the-sea homage I didn't run into them, although I did meet some Swedes, who were there to see how a barbecue contest is run before starting one of their own (a scary thought). I was disappointed not to see a single Elvis impersonator. On the other hand, there were very few politicians, considering the season, and there were no street mimes at all.

In the ninety-degree Memphis heat, female attire ran to halter-tops and cutoffs, often decorated with stickers saying things like "HOT," "Can't Touch This," "Roman Hands," and "USDA Choice," lovingly applied to passing butts by freelance inspectors in pig noses. I couldn't help but think of a recent, grim "feminist-vegetarian" monograph called *The Sexual Politics of Meat*. Dropped here by the banks of the Mississippi, its poor author would probably have been carried off gibbering. As a matter of fact, pig people seem to be politically incorrect on just about every score. A column in the *National Barbecue News*, for example, urged compassion for those who suffer from HIV—high intake of vegetables.

Some men wore overalls, Western clothes, or biker gear, but most wore shorts and T-shirts, often revealing all too plainly what beer and barbecue can do to the male physique. Overdressed and hot in the khakis and seersucker I'd worn on the plane, I reflected that those of us from Back East have to uphold standards, but welcomed the frequent spritzes from the water guns of good-natured party animals.

At the judges' tent we encountered a man with rows of rib bones worn on his chest like decorations. Given the atrocious puns I'd already been subjected to, I didn't have to ask (rib bones = ribbons, of course). He was dispensing stale barbecue wisdom, like "Both the pork and the cook should be well basted." My judicial duties wouldn't begin until the next day, so my sister and I set off to take in the showmanship competition.

"Showmanship" was judged on the basis of musical routines with barbecue and Italian themes, and the strongest entries came from teams of corporation or government agency employees who brought a sort of office-party atmosphere to the proceedings. "White boys can't dance," my sister muttered, as we watched one of these efforts. I reminded her that black ones probably couldn't either after drinking as much beer as some of these guys had. Shoot, they were doing pretty well to stand.

A group from South Central Bell presented a typical offering. Set in "Mama Bella's Pizzeria," it began with a grape-stomping number, followed by "Smoke Gets in Your Eyes" ("They asked me how I knew / I'd be barbecue"), a fine "Barbara Ann" take-off ("You got me smokin' and a-grillin' / Sauce will be a-spillin' / Barbecue"), three girls singing "Where the Boars Are," and a mildly risqué send-up of the old Platters number "Only You (Can Be My Barbecue)." At the end the whole cast joined in a dance number inspired by the idea of barbecue pizza. Inevitably, several other skits celebrated this concoction, which I gather is actually served as a regular thing at one Memphis restaurant. (I ate some at the judges' reception and it's not quite as vile as it sounds.)

Alas, the showmanship we saw was rather tame—nothing to match M. C. Hamhock. For genuine unglued weirdness we had to wait until that evening, when the featured act on the big stage turned out to be none other than my old Raleigh buddy the Reverend Billy C. Wirtz, down from Nashville where he moved a while back to pursue his dream. An audience of several thousand rowdy Southern pork-eaters sat rapt as Billy regaled us with a song about a truck-driving lesbian from outer space and other products of his off-center mind. After the show I introduced Billy to my sister, and he took us back to his van, where he gave us each a bottle of snake oil. The end to a perfect day. And the serious business of the contest—judging the pork—hadn't even begun.

Judgment Day

Did you notice how in 1992 the national media—the *New York Times,
Newsweek*, NPR, all of them—almost simultaneously began talking
about "the Bubba vote"? I seriously doubt that many of these folks
had actually met Bubba, much less discussed politics with him, but
at the Memphis in May World Championship Barbecue Contest they
sure could have.

Just before I went to Memphis, I'd spent a couple of days in Washington, reading college professors' grant applications at the National
Endowment for the Humanities. Imagine, if you can, leaving earnest
consideration of such subjects as how texts reflect and resist the
emergence of information as the form capital takes in the signifying
environment to go hang out with the Porkaholic Beefbusters, ZZ
Chop, and Pap-Paw's Pig Pokers as they deconstructed pigs, drank
beer, and raised hell. I don't like to brag, but a lesser man would
have suffered cultural whiplash.

Yeah, Bubba was there in force. And Tyrone was, too. (I don't
think that piece of shorthand's going to catch on with NPR, do you?)
Southern barbecue has always been a fine, biracial, working-class
enterprise, and it still is. In Memphis, private teams were mostly all-
black or all-white, but there were plenty of each, and the spectators
and some corporate and government teams were unselfconsciously
salt-and-pepper. We all sweltered together cheerfully in the ninety-
degree heat.

But I wasn't there as a mere tourist. No, sir. I had been invited
to judge the barbecue. So that evening, while the competitors were
applying mysterious dry-rubs to their meat and getting the coals
just right for a long night of cooking, I headed for the Orpheum,
a splendidly restored old downtown movie theater, for an orientation
meeting and reception.

As I strolled up Beale Street, I reflected that there's something
synthetic now, and a little sad, about Memphis's most famous boulevard. Urban renewal has turned it into a sort of Potemkin village,
three or four blocks of downtown storefronts surrounded by acres
of parking lots. Several clubs, including a new one owned by the
great B. B. King, offer genuinely good blues, but the neighborhood's tradition has been demolished almost as thoroughly as its
architecture.

From the Convention Bureau's point of view, of course, that may be just as well. The original Beale Street would have been hard to market to most out-of-towners, because its whole point was that it was a *Negro* street, the heart of black Memphis under Jim Crow. When Elvis came to Lansky's store to buy his first sharp threads, he was making more than a fashion statement. But that time has passed and if urban renewal hadn't killed the old Beale, the end of segregation probably would have, just the way it killed black business districts in other Southern towns. Schwab's department store is still in business, which is something, but its window is full of tourist souvenirs.

In the absence of a living tradition, Beale Street's entrepreneurs now try to emulate New Orleans. Since my last visit the blues clubs and obscene-T-shirt vendors had been joined by oyster bars, beignet stands, and converted Slurpee machines spewing frozen daiquiris into paper go-cups. There aren't enough drag queens yet, but my sister says they're working on it. Memphis probably needs to import some Louisiana Catholics, too: Beale Street's borderline-desperate Are-we-having-fun-yet? atmosphere feels mighty Protestant to me.

Anyway, I'd been feeling pretty smug about getting picked as a judge, but when I got to the theater I found that the honor was spread pretty thin: a couple of hundred other judges were already there. As the seats filled up, I checked out my colleagues. Some of the black folks were dressed to the nines, but shorts, T-shirts, and gimme caps seemed to be the uniform of the day for white boys. I was almost the only one in a coat and tie, the overdressed eastern dude again.

As we waited, I listened to some of my judicial brethren—guys from Kentucky and Alabama and a North Carolinian from the great barbecue town of Lexington—discuss other contests they had judged. One told me that he had completed a judge-training course offered by something called the Sanctioned Barbecue Contest Network, which sponsors some thirty major contests a year. Lord knows how many bootleg, minor-league contests there are, but the schedules in a fat newspaper called *National Barbecue News* suggest that there are enough to keep you busy most weekends if you're inclined that way. (Later, talking to some of the contestants, I discovered that some folks are. Americans can make a way of life out of some of the damnedest things, can't we?)

Listening to these guys, I began to wonder if I was out of my depth, but I was reassured when the orientation began. Obviously I wasn't the only novice. Our instructor began with the basics ("If you don't eat pork, please let us know") and moved on to matters of deportment ("Stay sober until *after* the judging") and ethics ("If your ex-wife's boyfriend is on a team, you should disqualify yourself"). He told us that prizes had already been given for the best "area," for hog-calling, for showmanship, and for something called the "Miss Piggy in Italy" contest. (One team's Miss Piggy, I read in the paper, was provided with an honor guard of Bacchae from the International Barbecue Bikini Team.) There were also prizes in a category for "other meats," which included everything from exotica like gator, snake, rabbit, and ostrich to chicken and beef (sorry about that, Texans). We were given to understand, however, that we were the elite: judges of barbecue, which starts with B, and that rhymes with P, and that stands for *pork.*

We were introduced to the rating scheme, told what to look for in the meat and sauce, and warned not to be impressed by how much money teams had spent on their areas, cookers, or uniforms. Our instructor explained why there were so many of us. There were nearly two hundred teams, he said, some with entries in more than one of the three divisions (ribs, shoulder, or whole-hog). Each entry was to be judged by six of us, and each judge was to judge only three to six entries, because you don't want your barbecue judged by someone whose taste buds have already been seared by the competition.

Fair enough. I was as ready as I was going to be.

The next morning I found the headquarters tent, checked in, and put on my special apron and judge's badge. I was to be a rib judge, and "on-site," as opposed to "blind." Each on-site judge was assigned a keeper: mine was a pleasant lady from Memphis who had done this several times before. Her job was to get me to the right places at the right times, and incidentally to rate my performance as a judge (sobriety counts, I gathered). Waiting nervously for the tasting to begin, I talked with another judge, a man from Boston down for his seventh Memphis contest. He had taken up barbecuing to impress a girlfriend whose previous beau had been a Southerner, he said, and he assured me that he now produces the best barbecue in Massachusetts and upstate New York, which (he added modestly) ain't saying much.

At last the signal came to begin the judging. As the blind judges went into their tent, where the platters were arriving, the rest of us were led off to begin our tasting. All the fun and games, Miss Piggy and all the rest, were irrelevant now. We were down where the pork meets the palate.

Well, I'll cut this short: the worst I had was good, but the best—cooked by a team called the Rowdy Southern Swine, from Kossuth, Mississippi—was out of this world. The smell of the smoked pork made my mouth water. When I picked up a rib and examined it, as instructed, I saw a crisp brown crust over moist tender meat, pink from smoking, the color even from end to end. The meat came easily off the bone, but kept its integrity (none of the mushiness that comes from parboiling). This meat had been cooked with dry, cool smoke, and lots of patience. A dry rub sealed in the juices, but most of the fat had long since melted and dripped away. The rib tasted as good as it smelled: sweet and smokey; crunchy, chewy, and melt-in-your-mouth, all at the same time.

And the sauces . . . Well, after a quarter-century in Chapel Hill I've become fond of simple vinegar and red pepper. East Carolina Minimalism. It respects the meat. But, oh my goodness, there's a lot to be said for Overmountain Baroque, too—except you can't say it without sounding like an ad in *Southern Living:*

> A symphony of Southern flavors: tart Sea Island tomatoes, mellow onions from Vidalia, sweet-and-sour molasses from Louisiana cane fields, and the Latin kick of peppers from South Texas. A sauce the color of Tennessee clay, with the fiery heat of an Alabama afternoon and the long slow sweetness of a Kentucky evening.

Or, worse, like a wine critic:

> A sauce of great character and finesse. Bright claret color, with a complex peppery nose. Lusty full-bodied taste: tomato catsup and chili the principal notes, with a definite garlic background and hints of—could it be grape jelly? Balance sustained throughout. An assertive finish and a pronounced afterburn.

I just made all that up, actually, except for the grape jelly, which I'll bet anything was the secret ingredient in one sauce I tasted. And why not? Applesauce isn't the only fruit that goes well with pork.

Anyway, I was pleased to find that I could discriminate intelligently among several first-rate plates of ribs. After I'd filled out my rating forms, I went back to two of the teams for second helpings and for the beer that I'd turned down earlier, with an eye on my keeper. I also had a pleasant chat with the Kossuth D.A.: small-town Southern lawyers generally know their barbecue.

I had a date for supper with my sister that evening (just a salad, thank you), so I missed the announcement of the winners, but the next morning's *Commercial Appeal* reported that the championship in the ribs division and overall Grand Championship had gone to a team from—well, from Illinois, of all places. It was no accident, either: the same guys had won two years earlier. They graciously pointed out that they come from Murphysboro, only thirty-five miles north of the Mason-Dixon line, and you have to admire them for going back to basics (no high-tech cooker, just concrete blocks with a grate and a piece of sheet metal to hold the smoke in). But, still, from *Illinois!*

It just goes to show what Yankees can do when they put their minds to it. But I'll bet the Rowdy Southern Swine had more fun.

Race Politics, Part 1

Two races were in progress on Sunday, September 6, 1992: the quadrennial presidential election and the 43rd annual Mountain Dew Southern 500 NASCAR Winston Cup Series Race. You probably noticed that Bill Clinton won the first, and real men will know that Darrell Waltrip won the second, but there's a connection that you may not be aware of. It was at the Darlington Raceway that Sunday that I finally realized that George Bush was in serious trouble.

Although I grew up twenty miles from the NASCAR track in Bristol, this was the first stock-car race I'd ever been to. When I was a lad, racing had an image problem—and not just an image problem. A very funny novel called *Stand on It* describes the drivers of my youth: "Fact of life: southern stock car drivers are mean bastards and they have dirt under their fingernails and chickenshit on the bottoms of their boots. The backs of their necks are red. They race all day and drink all night and screw a little on the side. Plus a lot of interpretive fighting with tire irons. It's their form of ballet."

And fans were cut from the same cloth: "Every other one has a wooden match in the corner of his mouth and a bottle in a brown paper bag between his feet. They are fine when the race starts—I suppose. By maybe the 250-mile mark they are all liquored up and the safest place to be is upside down out there on the goddam track."

A chubby, bespectacled teenager survives by knowing where not to go, so I reached midlife familiar with racing only at second hand, from more adventurous friends, from forgettable drive-in movies with titles like *Redline 7,000* and *Thunder Over Carolina*, and from Tom Wolfe's classic 1965 article about Junior Johnson, "The Last American Hero" (which, incidentally, introduced the Southern phrase "good old boy" to the rest of the world). Besides, the sport itself didn't interest me much. From time to time I ran across race coverage on the radio, but listening to it seemed about as pointless as listening to bowling. And racing wasn't much better on television: 'round and around and around and around we go, as Chubby Checker puts it.

But someone who purports to know the South needs to know the NASCAR scene, so I jumped at the chance to go to Darlington with my buddy Fetzer, who has been going for many years and has even written about it once or twice. At the crack of dawn on race day, he and I set off for South Carolina, he pointing out such sights along the way as Eunice's Grocery ("Home of Flat Nose, the World's Only Tree Climbing Dog") and a combination house of prostitution and—well, I'd better not say, but you'd never guess. We pulled into the town of Darlington about the time the hungover Saturday-night infield revelers were waking up and popping their first beers of the morning, and we went with the flow of traffic down a commercial strip, past Southland Gun Works and a crane set up for bungee-jumping, to the press office just across the road from the track. There we picked up our credentials. Yes, I was impersonating a journalist. In my defense let me say that grandstand admission ran fifty to one hundred dollars.

I drove through a tunnel under the grandstand and across the track (strongly tempted to hang a right and take a lap just for the hell of it) to the infield, which was a clutter of campers and trailers and converted buses, many of them with platforms on top for viewing the race. Scores of flags flapped in the breeze, enough rebel ones to

give the encampment the look of a lost Confederate regiment, but
also plenty of U.S. flags, plus the flags of many states, flags with
the colors of favorite drivers, and flags featuring portraits of Hank
Williams Jr. and Elvis. The folks in the infield had paid upwards of
$200 to park their vehicles and hook up to utilities, plus about $30
a head. I began to figure: 95,000 fans at these prices, plus television
and radio coverage, commercial sponsors' logos on everything in
sight. . . . Big bucks. And this was just one of thirty or so races in
a season that started at Daytona in February and wouldn't end until
November, in Atlanta.

We parked the car at the Goody's Headache Powder Media Center
(free Goody's, Pepsi, Slim Jims, Winstons, Texaco ballpoint pens,
sunscreen, chewing gum—this journalist business is all right). We
picked up a wad of press releases and set out for a walking tour of the
infield. A nearby concession area offered a mobile bank machine and
booths selling T-shirts, caps, patches, pork skin, hush puppies, and
$85 sunglasses. There were also toilets labeled "Men" and "Ladies"
(think about that), and for once the men's room line was longer—not
surprising since by my rough count male fans outnumbered female
ones by seven or eight to one.

I must say this was not because women were unwelcome or un-
appreciated, especially those in tight cutoffs and haltertops. Despite
the high testosterone level, however, most fans were subdued, sitting
quietly by their campers and drinking beer, waiting for the race to
start. Some were listening to country music, one or two to gospel; it
was Sunday morning, after all. We saw only one half-hearted fistfight.
The night before had been party time, but Fetzer said that even on
Saturday night things now aren't what they used to be (or what they
still are at, say, Talladega, where the police enter the infield only in
platoon strength). "They're afraid they'll scratch their Winnebagos"
was his scornful explanation.

Being journalists, we interviewed some of the fans. Most were
blue-collar guys from the South, although we talked to groups from
Michigan, Pennsylvania, and upstate New York. Most wore caps and
T-shirts with the logos of their favorite teams and drivers. All were
white. (The only black fan we encountered was a large guy in a
cowboy hat who was with a couple of similarly attired white buddies;

all the other black folks I saw were armed: security guards employed by the track.) We talked about where they'd come from, which drivers they were pulling for and why, and politics.

The last subject came naturally. Governor Clinton was coming in shortly to be the race's Grand Marshal, the first Democrat who had dared to show his face at Darlington since Jimmy Carter in 1976. Carter had been well received then, but in 1992 Clinton couldn't find a driver or owner or chief mechanic willing to introduce him around the garage area, and few fans were ready to embrace the Arkansas Boy Wonder, either. One fellow said he came to the races (from Pittsburgh) to get away from politics. "Politics should stay the hell out of it. Clinton, too." He was with five friends: among them the six had five favorite drivers, but all had been for Ross Perot, who had recently withdrawn from the race. Now they either were for Bush or were planning to sit it out. I told the one about how fast Arkansas women are (so fast they had to put a governor on them), and it was well received, if I do say so myself.

But it wasn't surprising that folks didn't like Clinton. Among race fans, the national Democratic Party is thoroughly discredited, about as popular as Honda or Toyota. The actual *news* was that many of those we talked to were undecided, and it looked as if Perot could have swept the field if he hadn't pulled out. We even found a few who planned to vote Democratic—outnumbered better than two to one and a little defensive about it, but solid in their choice. Most were distressed about "the economy," especially about unemployment, but a couple were, in their own peculiar way, pro-choice. "If some old gal gets knocked up, I don't want to hear about it" is how one put it. (Incidentally, true race fans will be amused to hear that the black, orange, and white colors of Dale Earnhardt, "Black #3," turned out to be an infallible political indicator. Pulling for Earnhardt is something like pulling for the old Oakland Raiders, and *none* of his fans was for Clinton. Not one.)

Anyway, as I said, Darlington would have been a tough crowd for any Democrat. Four years earlier Fetzer had talked to a hundred fans at the Southern 500; in an article I swiped my title from, he reported that ninety-nine planned to vote Republican, and only one yellow-dog Democrat was for Dukakis. No, if George Bush couldn't count on this crowd, he really was in deep doo-doo.

Welcome to Darlington. The cradle of southern stock car racing.
The sport was born near here the first time a U.S. Revenue agent
figured that he could catch a moonshiner running along a twisty
back road with a car load of booze. No way. . . . Darlington is
tradition. First of the big tracks in the Southland, the granddaddy
of them all. The land of racing heroes.

*Race
Politics,
Part 2*

—from *Stand on It*, by "Stroker Ace"

The morning of the 43rd annual Southern 500 found me and
my buddy Fetzer hanging out at Darlington Raceway, posing as
journalists. We talked to fans about the upcoming stock-car race,
and also about the upcoming presidential race (a contest that most
seemed to be trying to forget). I learned, first, that the circus factions
of Old Byzantium had nothing on the rivalry between the partisans
of Ford and Chevrolet and, second, that George Bush was in trouble.

Bush had about a two-to-one edge among those we talked to,
and a third or so were undecided, but that wasn't good enough for
what should have been a solidly anti-Democrat, if not pro-Republican,
crowd, one that had gone literally ninety-nine to one for Bush over
Dukakis four years earlier. We didn't run into anyone who was
actually unemployed (they couldn't have afforded the steep admission
prices), but the subject was on people's minds. What we heard too
often for Bush's comfort was encapsulated as the chorus of a country
song a few weeks later: "Saddam Hussein still has a job, but I don't."
Since Ross Perot was temporarily not in the running, that left Bill
Clinton, but there wasn't much enthusiasm for him either. In a couple
of hours Clinton would serve as the Southern 500's Grand Marshal,
facing what he must have known would be a hostile crowd, and I
admit I gave him a little grudging admiration for not calling in sick.

After we finished our informal poll, we went on to the garage
area, where hoi polloi like Clinton were not allowed (he couldn't
find an owner or driver willing to introduce him). Breezing past the
crowd pressed up against the chain-link fence hoping for a glimpse
of the drivers, we held out our press credentials and tried to look
authentically nonchalant and arrogant. It must have worked, because
the guard waved us through. Inside, powerful unmuffled engines
roared, and men in bright primary colors bent over and crawled

under matching-colored Fords, Chevrolets, and Pontiacs, plastered with commercial sponsors' insignia. The cars looked larger than life, and certainly they were larger than the Toyotas, Hondas, and BMWs that have pretty much taken their places on the streets where I come from. My buddy took a chaw of tobacco, and we stood watching, talking with some other onlookers about the threatening weather, yelling at each other over the blats and roars of the engines.

As the mechanics began to roll the cars out to their starting positions, we spied a crowd gathering and went over to see what was up. It was a chapel service, a regular feature of these races, conducted by a full-time itinerant NASCAR chaplain. We stood with the drivers and mechanics and their families as the preacher led us in song ("God is so good to me," "He saved my soul," "He's coming soon"), read a Bible passage, and delivered a little homily. It was only later, after I saw what racing looks like up close and began really to understand the danger and skill and luck it involves, that I thought of bullfighters praying before a fight.

After the service, we left the garage area, walked through a tunnel under the track, and rode an elevator to the press box beside the grandstand, where we took a couple of empty seats and helped ourselves to some of the free goodies provided for the "media." We were settling in to eat the free lunch when a NASCAR PR man asked to see our credentials, which turned out not to be potent enough for that. Asked politely to leave, we politely left, to find that in the meantime we'd missed the inferior cold cuts at the infield Media Center. One of the regular NASCAR reporters told us there were hot dogs at the Clinton-Gore trailer, but things were starting to happen on the stage facing the grandstand, so we scurried over to watch, pausing on the way to shake hands with Strom Thurmond, straw-hatted against the sun and working the crowd even though he wouldn't be up for reelection any time soon.

On the platform Governor Campbell of South Carolina introduced the legendary driver Richard Petty, who was making his last South Carolina race. Every mention of Petty's name evoked cheers and applause from the otherwise thoroughly indifferent crowd. Petty stood there, lean and mean in shades and a cowboy hat, smiling beatifically as the governor proclaimed Richard Petty Day and awarded him the Order of the Palmetto.

A couple of months later, when Petty was fixing to run the Hooters
500 in Atlanta—his last race, period—CBS television, for no apparent
reason, sent a crew around to ask me to comment on his status as
a Southern cultural icon. The Yankee interviewer kept asking why
King Richard is so admired in the South, and I tried to tell him,
but he didn't seem to like what I said. Anyway, he kept rephrasing
the question. I finally figured out that he wanted me to say that we
like Petty because we lost the Civil War and he gives us something
to be proud of. But I wasn't going to say *that*. I mean, (1) we're
not stupid enough to believe that anyone will think better of us for
having good stock-car drivers, (2) Southerners who are looking for
something to be proud of are found in Atlanta fern-bars, not at the
Darlington Raceway, and (3) I'm not sure that most race fans are
aware that we lost the war.

I felt so uneasy about the interview that I didn't watch the news
that night. Some of my friends said the next day that they caught
me pontificating on national TV, but it's interesting that none of
them can remember what I said. I hope it was that white Southern
working-class folk admire Petty because he has qualities that white
Southern working-class folk admire—like skill, courage, humility,
and sly humor.

Anyway, soon after Petty left to go get in his car there was a
commotion behind us as Clinton, his handlers, gofers, and accompa-
nying press showed up. From thirty feet away Clinton looked much
fatter than I'd thought, almost Kennedyesque. I was startled, until
it occurred to me that he probably had a bullet-proof vest under
his pullover sport shirt. For his sake, I hoped so: despite the Secret
Service men glaring from behind their sunglasses, 20,000 of us or so
had a clear shot, and nobody'd checked *me* for weapons. During the
invocation and national anthem, the crowd fell silent and removed
their hats for probably the only time that day. Most of the Clinton
press kept right on chatting and jockeying for camera angles, but I was
pleased to see Al May of the *Atlanta Journal-Constitution* uncover
and pay attention.

During all this, an airplane circled overhead towing a banner that
read "NO DRAFT DODGER FOR PRESIDENT," and when Clinton
was introduced he was roundly booed, to the obvious distress of the
reporters we were standing with. I noticed, however, that the boos

were more heartfelt than the chant of "Bush! Bush! Bush!" that a few people tried to start. Clinton, his glued-on smile unbroken, shouted the traditional "Gentlemen, start your engines" over the jeers and catcalls, and beat a hasty retreat as the mighty machines rolled out behind the pace car, engines throbbing and growling. They circled the track at highway speed; then at the green flag, with an unimaginable blast of engine noise, took off.

There are better places than here to read about racing, and better-informed writers to tell you about it. I'll just say that I now begin to understand the appeal of the sport. As the author of *Stand on It* puts it, "This is so different from racing Indy-type cars you can't believe it. There are folks who wet their pants every time they hear one of these big bastard NASCAR machines roar to life." The noise, the speed, the vivid colors, the pit crews' feverish work—all of this has a visceral appeal to anyone whose inner child is an East Tennessee sixteen-year-old. When those mighty cars are screaming past you 20 feet away at 150 miles an hour you truly appreciate the bravery of the drivers, whose skill and preparation are the only things standing between them and death. It takes a real hero—no kidding—to go out and face that every weekend, and to do it with the self-deprecating insouciance so characteristic of these men. (From *Stand on It*, again, Sam Bisby's Law: "It is useless to step on the brakes when your car is upside down.")

We watched enthralled for a time, then figured we'd better get back to work (and forage for lunch), so we nipped over to the Clinton-Gore compound to cop some hot dogs and see what the Democrats were up to. The compound consisted of a couple of trailers surrounded by chain-link fence, guarded by several burly security men in ties and gimme caps. The Clintonites, still waiting for their candidate to come shake hands, included a couple of Junior-Leaguey matrons and a male sociology professor from a nearby college, and they all looked seriously out of their element. The reporters traveling with Clinton were not a down-home crowd either (unlike the sports reporters we'd been hanging out with in the Media Center). Most had beat a path straight back to the campaign's air-conditioned trailer, where one took posterboard and markers and made a sign that said "Make Love Not Stockcar Races." Inside they pecked away on laptops and used the phone bank to file their stories about the candidate's chilly reception, which really did puzzle them. Fetzer and I, ever helpful, tried to explain to some that the real story was that not everybody had been booing. Sure, nobody was taking Clinton's bumper stickers or buying the $10 T-shirts, but nobody was firebombing the trailer, either. We told them that was bad news for Bush, but they didn't seem to believe us.

Back outside, I talked with some high school girls from Hartsville who had been recruited to work for the Clinton team, but had little to do and were sitting unhappily in the shade ignoring the cars hurtling past a hundred yards away. Yelling over the noise, I asked one if she'd ever been to a stock-car race before. No, she said. Would she ever come to one again? No way.

Fetzer and I gobbled our hot dogs, figuring we'd probably be paying for them for the next four years, and went off for one last look at the infield crowd, most of them now perched on top of their trailers and vans, studying the race intently. A complete 500-mile race would require 367 laps of the oval track, four hours or so, but the intricate Winston Cup scoring system awards points for a great many things besides where you finish, and there's always the possibility of a collision to keep the fans attentive.

I confess that we left early, after nearly three hours, with an eye on the gathering storm clouds and a desire to get away before the other 95,000 decided to do the same. We were headed back for North Carolina when we heard on the car radio that rain had stopped the race, at least temporarily. A couple of hours later we were drinking beer in a tavern in Wadesboro, talking with a bail bondsman and watching some of his clients play bumper pool, when the television johnnies interrupted their interviews with drivers and mechanics to announce that the race had been called for good. The bumper pool game stopped and we all turned our attention to the television for the final wrap-up.

Most of the discussion centered on the fact that Davey Allison had been in contention when the race was stopped. A victory for Allison would have added the "Winston Million" (a million dollars for anyone who wins three of the four most difficult races) to the $1.3 million he had already won in 1992. But Darrell Waltrip had gambled that the rain would begin and passed up a fuel stop, so he had been leading when the red flag came out and consequently won the race. Asked how much fuel he had left at the end, Waltrip grinned and said, "About a million dollars' worth."

A couple of months later, as you know, Bill Clinton was ahead when that other race was called.

Deo Vindice

One fall day I was visited by a couple of guys who were writing a cover story on the South for a Dutch magazine. They'd been to Darlington, Tuskegee, Oxford, Charleston, and other shrines of Southern culture, and I was pleased to see that Chapel Hill was still on the list. Over Allen & Son's barbecue we talked about their travels.

They'd just come from witnessing a War Between the States reenactment at Flat Rock, North Carolina, they said, and they were struck by the utter seriousness with which reenactors pursue their calling. It's an every-weekend event for many of them, with thousands of dollars spent on uniforms and equipment and travel to battles. My visitors were also impressed with the remarkable authenticity some of these weekend warriors achieve. Many refuse to do anything that their originals could not have done: they sleep on straw, cook vile food over open fires, huddle in leaky canvas tents against the rain.

But even in the most scrupulously nineteenth-century setting it seems that some contemporary issues just won't go away. My Dutch friends had met a young woman who's tired of being a camp follower and bandage roller, and wants to shoot it out with the boys. Women in the military, retroactively.

Now, historically, a few women really did bear arms for Southern independence. Harry Turtledove's remarkable science-fiction novel *The Guns of the South* makes use of the genuine case of Molly Bean, who fought for two years (and was twice wounded) with the 47th North Carolina. But I gather that Molly could pass for a man, or at least for a boy, and apparently that's not a possibility for this latter-day Janie Reb. She isn't letting that stop her, though: she's muttering about legal action—an option that probably wouldn't be open to her if the Confederacy had won.

Anyway, when I had to confess that, as a matter of fact, I'd never been to a reenactment, I could see my credibility rapidly evaporating.

So when I learned that the very next week there was to be one just down the road from us, I took it as a sign that the time had come for me to fill this hole in my experience. With three visiting English friends, my patient wife and I set off to see the little-known battle of Averasboro, originally fought in March of 1865.

As we pulled into the makeshift parking area, paid our five dollars to the Confederate-uniformed guard, and took a program from his hoop-skirted assistant, we could see the cantonment, which had been set up that morning. Various Confederate flags—the Stars and Bars, the Stainless Banner, the Battle Flag—fluttered in the breeze over a concession area offering refreshments, souvenirs, and bumper stickers saying things like "I'd Rather Be Shooting Yankees" and "Don't Blame Us: We Voted for Jefferson Davis." I bought a minié ball to go on my key ring, with the .45 cartridge that was already there. (The cartridge was a gift from the distinguished Southern poet Fred Chappell, who told me it's a mojo to keep liberals away, but mostly it just causes me problems in airports.)

We had missed the Gentlemen's Duel and the Period Fashion Show, but arrived just in time for the Capture and Trial of a Federal Spy, which the program said would take fifteen minutes—short work, we reckoned. The spy turned out to be a woman (not a lady, obviously), so Southern chivalry wouldn't allow her to face a firing squad on the spot. To our disappointment, she was just marched off under guard to prison in Raleigh.

Soon the cavalry came jingling by—a score of splendid horses, their riders in an authentically motley assortment of grey and butternut uniforms, most of them with plumed hats à la Jeb Stuart. They rode across the pasture-battlefield and into the woods, to reconnoiter for Sherman's forces, moving up from South Carolina. Meanwhile, the field artillery, distinguished by the red flashes on their natty grey uniforms (too natty for 1865, I thought), wheeled their big gun into place on a knoll overlooking the field. The infantry—fifty or sixty men, three young drummer boys, and a couple of officers— marched from the camp to the field, where they knelt for a prayer by the chaplain, then arrayed themselves in three trenches that looked suspiciously like the work of a modern backhoe. The regimental band had set up just down from the artillery, and it struck up a couple of hymns, then "Just before the Battle, Mother." Several hundred of us spectators were strung out on a line perpendicular to the trenches. Everything was in place. Now all we needed was some Yankees.

The public address announcer gave us a rundown on the battle we were about to observe: essentially a holding action late in the war, he said, nothing much in the way of strategic significance—in other words, a hell of a place to die, but some folks were fixing to, anyway.

Eventually the Confederate troopers galloped out of the woods to report the enemy's approach. Then a couple of Union horsemen were spotted, before they rode off to deliver *their* report. The crowd was getting restless. Suddenly, at the edge of the forest, there they were—the blue-belly hordes! Maybe twenty of them.

It seems there's a problem. Nobody wants to be a Yankee. Even the few who turned out on this afternoon didn't seem very enthusiastic about it. One of them said only, "It's a nasty job, but somebody's got to do it." I read later that reenactments of our civil war are a big deal in Europe, and that they have the same problem, but they've solved it with characteristic finesse: European reenactors are required to be Yankees for several years before they're allowed to be Confederates.

Anyway, back in North Carolina, the federals formed up in a double line and advanced across the open field toward the first of the three earthworks. This sort of suicidal advance (on a larger scale, of course) just about did in the Confederate army at Gettysburg, but when the artillery cut loose with a deafening "ka-booooom"—no one fell. The Confederates in the forward trench held their fire until the blue line was almost on them, then cut loose with a sheet of flame, a mighty "craa-aack," billows of black-powder smoke—and still no one fell. Just over the hill, I reminded myself, folks were waterskiing on Falls Lake, and I wondered what they made of all the gunfire.

With loud huzzas and bayonets fixed, the corporal's guard of Yanks (one of them in a dashing Zouave outfit) charged the trench, broke the green South Carolina militiamen who manned it, and drove them back, then went on to rout the second line and drive *them* back. Meanwhile, off to the side, the equally outnumbered Union horse-soldiers, sabres drawn, were mixing it up inconclusively with the rebel cavalry.

By this time dead and wounded Confederates littered the field, but the Yankee boys hadn't yet taken any casualties to speak of. We understood that this was because there weren't any Union soldiers to spare, but still, it was getting embarrassing. As the thin blue line advanced past the dead and dying Confederates toward the third and last of the Confederate trenches, I was reminded of what Reuben Greenberg, the black police chief of Charleston, South Carolina, said when someone asked why he gave one of his officers time off from work to march with the Palmetto Guards. "Well," Chief Greenberg said, "you all have always told me that one boy in grey is worth ten in blue." But it sure wasn't working out that way this particular afternoon, and the crowd was getting uneasy. When the sound of a jet plane was heard through the overcast, someone joked, "At last— air support!"

In the trench waited the rebs who had successfully withdrawn from the forward works and those who had been held in reserve all along. So far the Yankees had been invincible, but now at last they would be allowed to die for their country. From twenty feet away they took a volley head on. Then another. As the crowd cheered, they crumpled like tissue paper. Through all of this, the band had been playing jaunty airs. Now they struck up "Dixie," then "The Bonny Blue Flag." As the Confederates came out of the trench to recover their wounded, one paused to examine a fallen Yankee. "Take his shoes!" a woman next to me shouted.

Afterwards we wandered around the camp, where we watched the amiable fraternization between Blue and Grey. We bought some sarsaparilla, on tap at one of the sutlers' wagons, and looked around the hospital tent, where a medical student from East Carolina University had set up his array of antique bone-saws and other fearsome implements. Someone introduced me to Wolfgang Dresser, a young man who has achieved some fame in reenacting circles for his devotion to the Cause. Every year Herr Dresser comes over from Germany for a month's vacation, going from one reenactment to another, serving as a Confederate private. (What I want to know is, where were these guys when we needed them?)

My wife overheard one Confederate private telling another that there was a Pizza Hut a couple of miles down the road. When she said "Pizza Hut?" he grinned and, turning to his buddy, said, "Say, I saw me a dead mule back yonder. Looks like mighty good eatin' tonight!" Other rebels took their cuisine more seriously, however.

A naval unit up from the coast (with their boat on a trailer) was cooking cabbage and field peas in a big iron pot. The jolly jack tars had fought as infantry that day, but back in camp they were sailors again, and proudly showed us their guns and "torpedoes" (mines). They explained that everything on the boat was authentic except the modern life jackets and radio equipment required by the U.S. Coast Guard. I reflected that a Confederate Coast Guard probably wouldn't have meddled.

It was getting late and we were getting hungry (and for something better than cabbage and field peas), so our English friends bought one last souvenir and we hit the road. A good day's work. The Yankee advance had been thwarted, however temporarily. There was still hope.

At lunch a few days later with some academic folk, I was telling my companions about the afternoon, and how—well, *interesting* was the word my English friends had used, and that's exactly right—how *interesting* it was.

"I don't know," one of the others said. "Didn't you find it just a little—you know?"

Unfortunately I did, but I wanted to make him say it. I asked him what he meant.

"Well," he said, "wasn't it sort of a redneck crowd?"

I told him, first, not really, and, second, I don't have anything against rednecks, and we let the subject drop, by tacit mutual consent. But I wish I hadn't.

Look, what I saw was a bunch of guys out having a good time—shooting guns, riding horses, camping out, praying—and a few hundred citizens like me, who enjoyed watching them do it. Sure, most of the Confederate reenactors seemed to be Southern patriots, and many of them were doing homage to their ancestors. My questioner may have a problem with that, but I don't.

As for racism, which I take to be the real subtext of that question— well, one of my English friends was sniffing about for that, too. He was somewhat surprised by one woman's battle-flag T-shirt that said "Heritage, Not Hate," but his suspicions were confirmed when the PA announcer concluded a list of American wars with " . . . Korea,

169

*The
Mississippi
Hippies
and Other
Denizens
of the
Deep South*

Vietnam, the Persian Gulf, Los Angeles." He has been in American academic life long enough to know that opposition to burning and looting is just a mask for racism.

For my part, though, I was struck with the fact that my English friend had to do some decoding to conclude that we had fallen among bigots. I mean, when small-town and rural white Southerners have racist thoughts we're notorious for not keeping them to ourselves, and I didn't hear any overtly racist talk all day. I did hear some strictures directed at the junior senator from Illinois, but, after all, she started it.

No, the senator would not have been well received, in the unlikely event she had chosen to make an appearance that afternoon. On the other hand, while it's true (and to my mind perfectly unremarkable) that this was almost entirely a white crowd, I stood for a while near a middle-aged black man, who seemed to be having fun, like everybody else. If he was pulling for the Yankees he kept it to himself, but I don't believe he'd have taken more than good-natured teasing if he'd 'fessed up.

And I wouldn't have hesitated at all to introduce my friend Don to these guys. Don is a Mississippian, now a college professor up north, and he belongs to something called the Sable Arm, an organization with membership limited to direct descendants of black Union soldiers. He's not a reenactor, but some of his friends are. (Where do you think the 54th Massachusetts in the movie *Glory* came from?) If I had taken Don along that afternoon, I'm sure he would have been welcomed—kidded, perhaps, like the Union reenactors, but welcomed. And he'd have understood what was going on a good deal better than your average college professor.

The Mississippi Hippies and Other Denizens of the Deep South

January in Jackson—well, it wasn't April in Paris, but it had its pleasures, among them the chance to compare the Magnolia State to the more northerly South I know better. I was lecturing at Millsaps College, staying in a nearby motel with a view from my window of the quaint little observatory that figures in the delightful, made-in-Jackson movie *Miss Firecracker*. Millsaps is a small college with a good faculty, so its students may get worked a little harder than average, but campus life seems to be pretty much standard-issue Southern collegiate: "Inez-burgers" and beer at the student hangout, "meanbadboogie" by a group called the Mississippi Hippies, and so forth. The only thing that struck me as odd about Millsaps was its emphasis on security: the college is a heavily patrolled, fenced compound with only two entrances, both guarded after 6:00 P.M. Turns out there's a reason for that.

As the state capital, Jackson has picked up some of the accoutrements of yuppiedom—fern bars, fitness centers, even a bookstore good enough to stock my books. But these amenities coexist with concentrated poverty of a sort that you've got to get pretty far off the Interstates to find in North Carolina these days. Jackson's the first place outside the Third World, for instance, where I've seen cigarettes routinely sold one at a time. Within sight of its downtown office buildings are blocks of squalid shotgun houses adjoining old Farrish Street. Now that the black middle class has moved to the outskirts of town and patronizes the same malls as the white folks, the once-vibrant commercial district of Negro Jackson has become a shuttered, graffiti-scarred wasteland.

Take this, add the crack scourge amply documented on local television news shows, stir in some pockets of relative affluence like Millsaps, and you've got the ingredients for a serious crime problem. Razor wire sales are obviously booming, and burglar alarm systems and private security patrols seem to be increasingly ordinary expenses of middle-class life. Of course, Jackson's not unique in this respect (we had a drive-by shooting a half-block from my house in Chapel Hill recently), it's just that the contrasts are starker than I'm used to.

Most of the city's problems, including this one, are tied in one way or another with race, so it should be said on the city's behalf that relations between black and white folk strike a visitor as relatively amicable. My racial animosity sensors are in pretty good working order and I've detected more—both ways—in some single days in New York City than in a whole month in Jackson, 1993. Black and white Jacksonians alike were uniformly civil and usually more than that to me and, as far as I could see, to each other. A very important contributing factor has to be that the spokesmen for the black community (at least the ones I encountered) are serious, sober, and constructive.

*The
Mississippi
Hippies
and Other
Denizens
of the
Deep South*

One Jackson image that will stick with me is that of a disconcerting "ghost mall" not far from the college, abandoned when the surrounding residential districts changed their demographic complexion. Next to it was a billboard offering the Virgin Mary's 800 number in Bayside, Queens. (For some reason, the poorer sections of Jackson were blanketed with these signs. The local Catholic bishop took to the pages of the *Clarion-Ledger* to deny any connection between his diocese and this enterprise.) Across the street, in a security-gated hole in the wall, you can find Tony's Tamales, which I recommend. Tamales have long been traditional fare for black Mississippians, although no one has ever been able to tell me why.

Tamales aside, I figured culinary Jackson would be typically Southern: a meat and three vegetable plate–lunch town with an overlay of all-American fast food and a few pretentious expense-account joints where the waiters tote big pepper mills. I don't have to go to Mississippi for any of that, so I figured I'd eat Special K for a month, save some money, and lose the weight I had gained over Christmas. But I underestimated both the hospitality of Jacksonians and the quality of the restaurants they'd take me to.

Jackson does have good country cooking (try the restaurant at the Farmers Market). Midway between Memphis and New Orleans, it also has good ribs and passable muffeletas. But my favorite restaurant—and not just because I went there with Eudora Welty—has a sign out front that says "Bill's Burgers, God Bless America." In typical Mississippi fashion, its owner isn't named Bill and its specialty is seafood. Jackson's proximity to the Gulf means it has at least a half-dozen fine fish places, most of them run by Greeks like "Bill." The Mayflower is another, downtown near the capitol; a Jackson fixture for decades, it is run by a couple from Patmos.

One weekend I took a leisurely drive up through the Delta to Memphis. This rich bottomland between the Yazoo and Mississippi rivers is the subject of my friend Jim Cobb's fine book, *The Most Southern Place on Earth*, and by some criteria it may be that. Certainly it offers the largest concentration of rural black poverty in the United States, it has for over a hundred years, and the recent introduction of large-scale commercial catfish farming hasn't done much to change that. I once made fun of V. S. Naipaul's book on the South for overusing the "one could have been in" gimmick, but the Delta's semitropical landscape flat to the misty horizon, the ramshackle recycling of building materials, the gormless decoration with primary colors—well, one could have been in Nigeria.

The Delta has been fertile in so many ways. Even its place-names are rich in associations, few of them happy, and it has exported its children by the scores of thousands. My route took me first to Yazoo City, home of Willie Morris and lately both Clinton's secretary of agriculture and the chairman of the Republican National Committee. On to Indianola, home of B. B. King and the White Citizens Council. Past Parchman, the notorious state prison immortalized in a Mose Allison lyric ("Sittin' over here on Parchman Farm / I never did no man no harm / Gonna be here the rest of my life / And all I did was shoot my wife"). To Clarksdale, home of the Delta Blues Museum, and beyond, past Graceland, into Memphis. For the last part of the trip I was on old Highway 61, the way out to the North for countless black Mississippians and a good many white ones, too. Bill Ferris, director of the Center for the Study of Southern Culture at Ole Miss, has named his Saturday night public-radio blues program for this road. The Blues Doctor gets a lot of requests from Parchman.

Back in Jackson, one Sunday morning I went over to the state Agricultural and Forestry Museum, where stands a reconstructed Mississippi village of ca. 1920, differing from a good many hamlets still dotting the Southern countryside mostly by being tidier. In the old, unheated, white frame country church a small Anglican congregation gathers to worship by the Old Prayer Book. About twenty of us were there that morning, and I listened with pleasure to a sermon on the ideal of the gentleman, as limned in the Epistle to the Romans. After Communion, we adjourned to the old Masonic hall for coffee.

Another Sabbath found me at a very different service, at Jackson's First Presbyterian Church, where I went with my friends Douglas and Caroline, he a seminary professor, a proud Scot from North Carolina, she a high school Latin teacher, the daughter of a Cambridge don. Jackson is Baptist and Methodist country, but "First Pres" has several thousand members, a good proportion of them present that Sunday. The church has missionaries at work in the Delta, in Prague and Bratislava and the Ukraine, in London (among Muslims), and even in

New York City. The service we attended was videotaped for satellite broadcast to Canada.

That evening I watched another televised local ritual, a broadcast taped at the local "cowboy" club, Rodeo's, which draws even better than the Presbyterian church. Fifteen hundred dancing white people would be a scary sight under the best of circumstances, but when they're engaged in semi-aerobic boot-scootin' line dances with names like the Electric Slide and the Tush Push—well, I don't know. I confess that I've been to the Longbranch in Raleigh. I've even done the two-step there. But I've never seen the likes of this. All I have to say is: I don't think Hank done it this-a-way.

So many other impressions:

> An informative sociological tour of Jackson with a retired businessman who studied with Howard Odum and Rupert Vance at North Carolina in the 1930s and wrote his master's thesis on sharecropping. I was reminded of Chapel Hill's great and beneficent influence in those days, when the South's problems seemed to be simpler.

> The good little museum in the Old Capitol building, with its even-handed treatment of the state's often troubled past. On one of the building's splendid curving staircases, a stunning blonde in a bridal dress was being photographed.

> A Kappa Alpha "convivium," where Douglas, in a dinner jacket and the tartan of his clan, spoke on Robert E. Lee as a Christian gentleman. The Knights and their ladies concluded the evening with the traditional toast to the General, the "spiritual founder" of their Order, in pure water.

> A visit to Tougaloo College, a small black institution with a distinguished history through the civil rights movement, now sadly down at the heels, scrambling for federal funds, and seeking some coherent mission in the wake of that movement's success.

> A conference at the University of Mississippi in Oxford, where our tweedy group joined several hundred drunken undergraduates to hear a Memphis retro band called the Bouffants. Halfway through "Chain of Fools," C. Vann Woodward of Arkansas and

Yale, the dean of Southern historians, leaned over and shouted, "They're not bad."

All in all, I returned to North Carolina better informed, if not wiser. Yes, Mississippi is different from the upper South, but mostly just in the same ways that the upper South differs from, say, Massachusetts. The people are even more friendly, the Protestant churches are even more conspicuous, the homicide rate is even higher, the food has even more cholesterol, and so forth. Some of the differences are big, but not many are qualitative. Except perhaps in the Delta, I felt in some primal sense at home in Mississippi. W. J. Cash wrote fifty years ago, "If it can be said that there are many Souths, the fact remains that there is also one South." He was right about that.

Preaching a Revival

A humid Dixie evening in June, in a field outside Little Rock. A large tent slowly fills with a crowd of three hundred or so Arkansawyers, many of the men in poplin and seersucker, many women in cotton summer dresses. They sit in folding chairs and fan themselves, stirred no doubt by racial memories of revivals, political rallies, the Scopes trial.... Clouds of mosquitoes join us under the tent as a full moon rises over the bayou behind the platform.

Oh, all right. It was a pond, not a proper bayou. Still, we were there to debate the question "Is There Still a South?" I had the affirmative, and the setting was definitely on my side. The only discordant notes were the occasional strains of *Madame Butterfly* (in rehearsal at the nearby performing arts center) and the mysterious presence of twenty visiting Chinese students.

I had a worthy adversary in Hodding Carter III, scion of the Mississippi newspaper family and late spokesman for Jimmy Carter's State Department, who had recently published an essay in *Time* pronouncing the South's death. The third speaker was Professor Linda Reed, a black Alabamian who heads the African-American studies program at the University of Houston. I wasn't sure where she'd come down on this question. Our moderator was the witty and learned Arkansas newspaperman Paul Greenberg.

For weeks I had been boasting of this invitation to anyone who'd listen, probably sounding something like those pro wrestlers you see on TV: *"Thursday night! At Wildwood! In the cage match! I'm gonna mop the floor with Mr. Hodding Carter the third!"* (My daughter was taken with his name: "How can anybody named Hodding Carter III say there's no South?" she asked. Smart girl.) Of course at supper before the debate we joked and told stories—this is just show business— but as Greenberg introduced us, I felt the old Celtic blood-lust rising. I was to go first, Linda Reed second, Carter would bat clean-up.

Looking out over the crowd, I reflected that this was probably as close as I'd ever come to preaching a tent meeting, so I started with the story of the young minister being interviewed for his first pulpit. The interview was going well until one old deacon leaned back and asked, "Young man, do you believe in the seven-fold gifts of the Spirit?" "Yes, I do," the minister began—then, seeing some frowns around the room, he added, "but I can preach it either way."

That's the way I feel about the South, I said: I believe it still exists, but I can preach it either way. If I wanted to argue that it is no more, I'd point to the astonishing changes of the past fifty years. I might go out on a limb, I said, and venture that only a handful of those present knew whose birthday it was that evening. (This was risky, but my surmise was correct: only two in the audience knew that it was Jefferson Davis's.) Yep, things have sure changed in these parts, in ways that no one would have predicted and many would not have welcomed, not very long ago.

But, I acknowledged, I wasn't brought to preach it that way. I had come to refute Mr. Carter's infamous *Time* essay. That's easy.

I could simply remark that anyone from Greenville, Mississippi, who thinks there is no more South has lived in Washington too long. But, I said, that would be a cheap shot.

I could tell about driving north the week before, crossing the Mason-Dixon line and being greeted by a sign that said "Welcome to Pennsylvania / America Starts Here."

Or I could observe that our mere presence attested to the living reality of the South. I mean, would anyone come to a discussion of whether there's still a Midwest? Who cares? (I couldn't resist.) Yet millions care whether the South still stands. Many care passionately. And the reason is that *being Southern* is important to them. Now more than ever, men and women find themselves in circumstances that demand to know "Who are you?"—and for many, "a Southerner" is still part of the answer.

There's nothing strange or un-American about this. We're just one of the scores of cultures in the United States that find comfort in a group identity and resist, to some degree, the melting pot. I pointed out that it's even trendy: we were "multicultural" before that word got hot.

True, this sense of identity may now be based more on a shared cultural style than on shared problems or even a shared history. But its strength is evident even in something as seemingly trivial as the success of *Southern Living* magazine. That magazine's very title attests, first, that the South exists; second, that its way of living is different (different enough to need a separate magazine, at least)—and nearly three million Southern households endorse those propositions with their subscription checks.

But I asked my listeners to notice that *Southern Living* addresses an affluent and suburban South that didn't exist fifty years ago. A great many "Southern" things are in fact new things: kudzu, Wal-Mart, country music, fast-food ham biscuits, four-by-fours, tailgate parties, stock-car racing, shopping mall cafeterias, the Atlanta Braves, electronic fish-finders, TV evangelists—I could go on, but the point is simply that Southerners are continually finding new bottles for old wine, using new technologies, adapting to new circumstances.

Some important regional differences have disappeared, to be sure, but many still persist. I cited my book *The Enduring South* (a shameless plug). And where regional differences are decreasing, it's often because other Americans are changing to look like us. That's true, for instance, of homicide rates, tastes in music, and even possibly religion.

Given all this, here's what I said to Mr. Carter: You can *define* the South out of existence if you want to. You can say "the South" means a poor, rural region with lousy race relations, still fighting the War between the States. If you do that, then sure, the South is disappearing.

But thank God the South has been and is becoming something different. It still lives in the hearts and minds of Southerners, and not just there but on the ground. It still provides what C. Vann Woodward called an American counterpoint, still stands as (in W. J. Cash's phrase) not a nation but the next thing to it.

With that, I sat down, pleased with myself. My listeners were in a good mood, so they had laughed at stuff that doesn't look all that funny set down on paper. (Maybe you had to be there.) Also, they plainly agreed with me, as I should have guessed they would: anyone who'd pay to hear a debate on this topic would.

Linda Reed took the pulpit next, and she also agreed with me. One thing that has made and keeps the South different, she said, is the presence and contribution and influence of black folk. I was delighted that she emphasized this point. Mountain boys like me tend to understate it, but I can't argue with it, and wouldn't want to.

Finally it was Hodding Carter's turn. He stood, raised his arms to heaven, tears (or, more likely, sweat) streaming down his face, and wailed, "I have sinned! I repent! I acknowledge the error of my ways!" Then, as Greenberg put it afterwards, he made as good a case as can possibly be made for his essentially base and despicable position. His argument was pretty much the one I'd anticipated: that today's region wouldn't be recognized by the people who were defining the South when he graduated from Greenville High School in 1953.

He was right about that, of course, although it was more fun not to say so. Still, I reflected on the fact that the white patrician from the Delta says the South is over, while the Jew and the black and the hillbilly say it ain't. Lord knows which side the Chinese came down on, but the rest of the crowd was with us.

We took some questions from the audience (including one from an aggrieved Midwesterner), then adjourned, only a half-hour or so behind schedule, not bad for Southerners on a summer evening. Shaking hands afterwards, we all agreed that we had had a good time and had made some points worth making.

The next couple of days my wife and I kicked around Little Rock, taking in some of the city's charming turn-of-the-century neighborhoods. We saw, among other things, the house that figures in the opening scenes of *Designing Women*. One afternoon we drove to the decaying resort town of Hot Springs, where we ate lunch at McClard's, consensus All-American barbecue joint, and chatted with a fellow porciphile, visiting from Fort Smith for a Ray Charles concert. Then we headed downtown for a look at some of the grand old bathhouses, only one still in service, one maintained by the Park Service as a sort of museum of the golden age of hydrotherapy, the others all now padlocked. As we had a drink in the lobby of the splendid old Arlington Hotel with some folks in town for a poultry farmers' convention, I wished Hodding was with us. The South dead! Imagine!

About the Author

I have assembled here bits and pieces of the squibs that went with these essays when they were originally published. If by some chance you're curious about who wrote them, I guess there are some relevant facts in here. Alternatively, anyone who has a lot of time to kill can try to match phrases from below with the pieces they originally accompanied. If you know as much about the author as you care to and have better things to do with your time, God knows I understand.

Professor the Honorable John Shelton Reed, Ph.D., grew up in Kingsport, Tennessee, where Confederate flags are more common now than they were in 1861–1865. He lived for ten years in Massachusetts and New York, but has taught since 1969 at the University of North Carolina at Chapel Hill, when he hasn't been hanging out at conferences and symposia, or visiting places like Northern California (where sin is obsolete) and Jackson, Mississippi (where it isn't).

He isn't really a journalist, but he's willing to fake it. He has been interviewed by NPR twice, once on ice tea and once on mint juleps. (He muddles his mint.) An Episcopalian, he attends evensong at Christ Church whenever he is in Oxford, and he has written on the cultural politics of Victorian Anglo-Catholicism. He has two daughters, likes real Texans, and gets his exercise by not owning a remote control for his television. He drives a four-cylinder Plymouth Voyager, but it does have a manual transmission. He thought it was American-made, but learned too late that it was assembled in Canada.

Some of his best friends are vegetarians, and others are animals. He cooks a decent mess of ribs himself, however, and has never hugged a tree he wasn't climbing at the time. Politically, he considers himself a country-club Republican *manqué,* although his buddy Parnell once named a baby donkey after him. He supports domestic content legislation for the South and wants to re-ratify the Tenth Amendment, adding the words "and this time we really mean it." He hates to be called a "moderate," but he doesn't mean to criticize.